URBAN RAIN

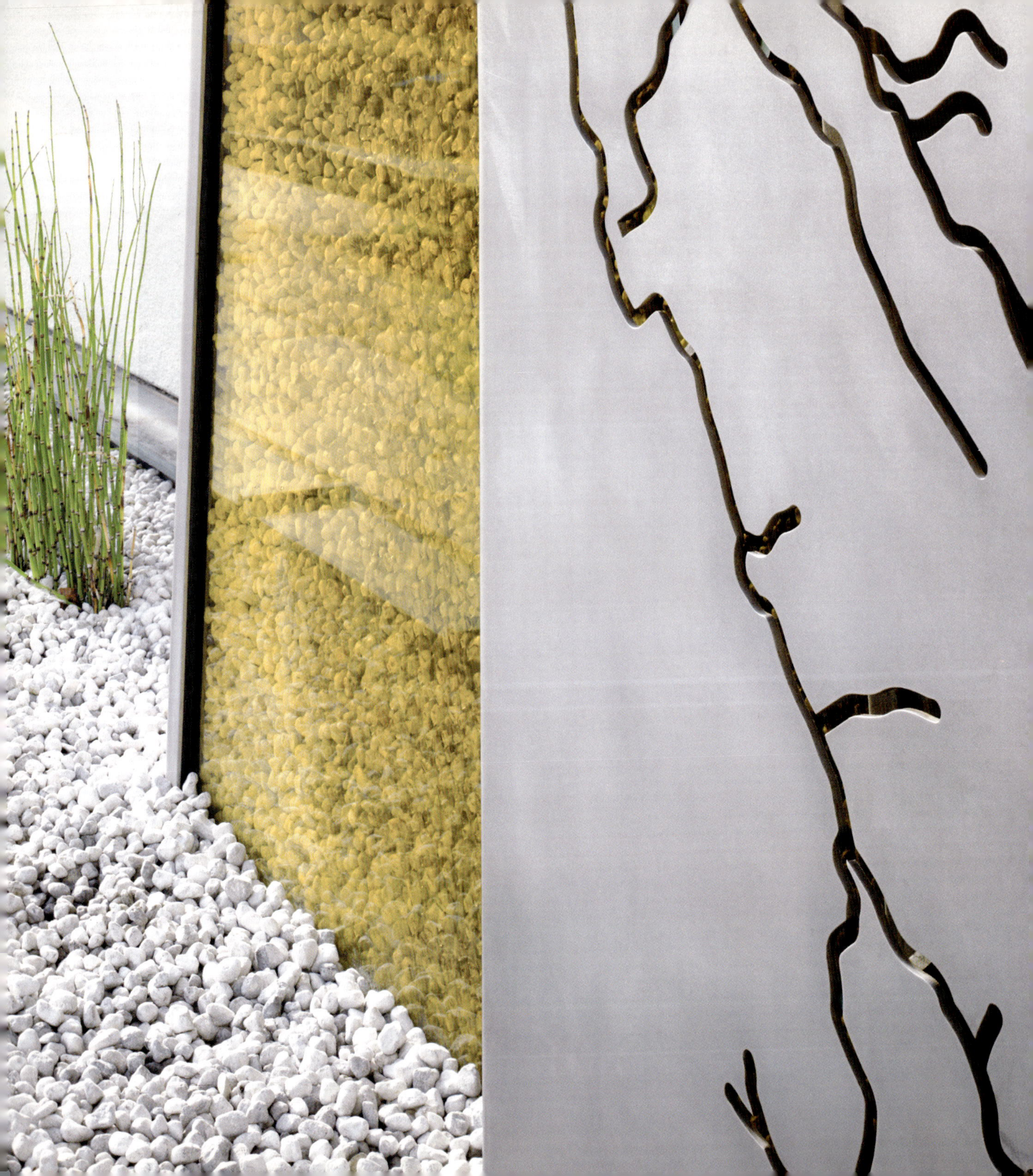

URBAN RAIN STORMWATER AS RESOURCE

ARTIST, JACKIE BROOKNER

A City of San Jose Public Art Project at Roosevelt Community Center

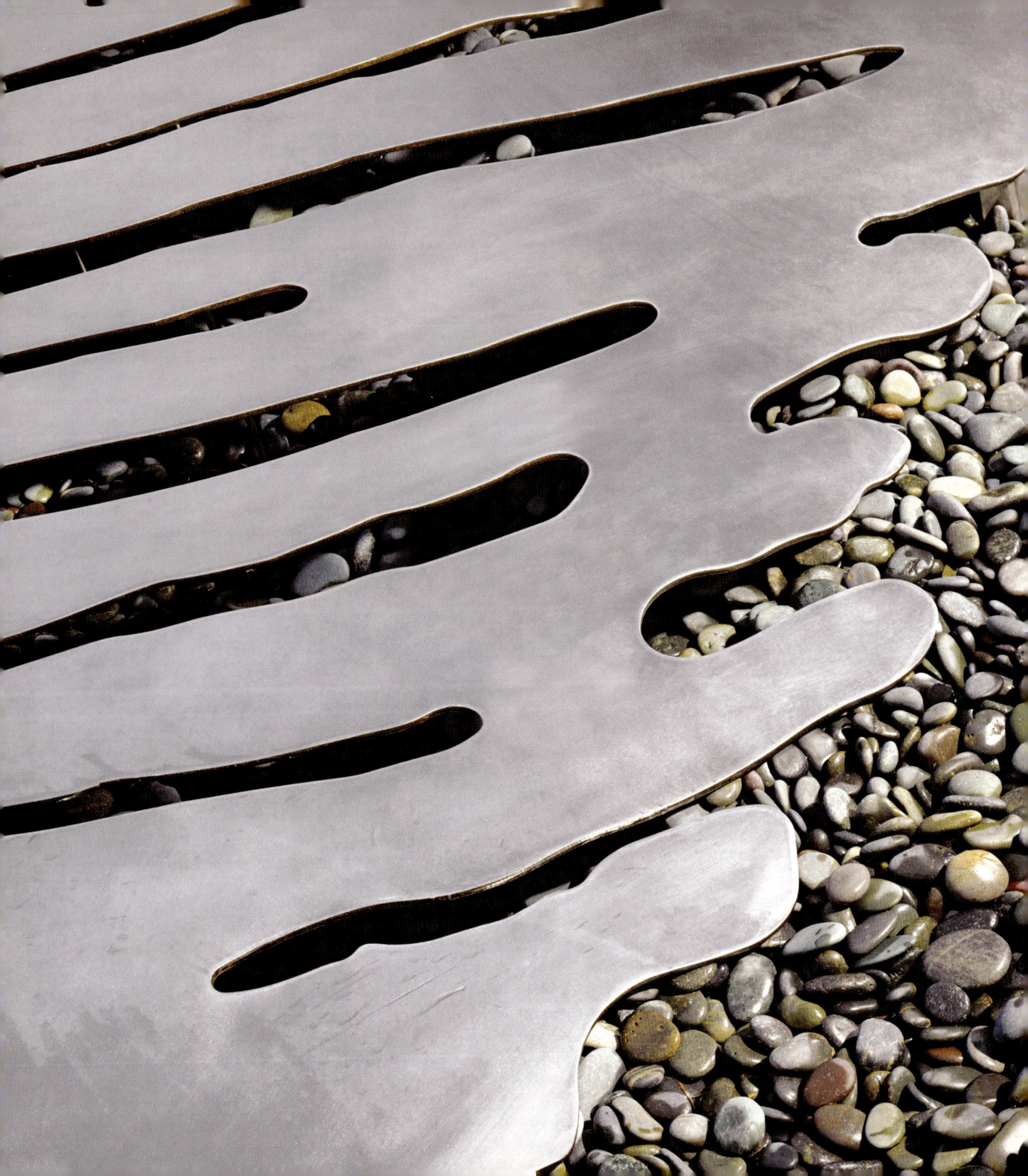

Roosevelt Community Center sits at the intersection of diverse cultures and ecologies. Located on the site of a former high school, amid several historic neighborhoods, across the street from a fast food restaurant and adjacent to Coyote Creek, the community center is ripe with local meaning. It is also a place that looks to the future. The center was designed to serve multiple generations with a strong focus on the needs of young people; and the building's sustainable design demonstrates the City's commitment to the future.

These factors came into focus with artist selection for the Roosevelt Community Center. Community members informed the artist selection process by establishing ambitious goals that included: art that would be recognizable, welcoming, inclusive, integrated into the building and landscape, related to Coyote Creek and neighborhood history, sustainable, and appealing to young people. Drawing from these goals, San Jose Public Art staff reviewed its artist roster and created a short list of artists for consideration. Community members then selected two artists to design site-integrated art at the Community Center—Scape (Edward) Martinez, a local urban artist who created a series of elaborate and colorful wall surfaces and sculpture, and Jackie Brookner, an established environmental artist whose work addressed the building's green goals.

Jackie Brookner worked collaboratively with the G4 Architects and Environmental Services Department staff to design artwork that would demonstrate the capture of stormwater and become an integral part of the building's green systems. Based on Brookner's proposals, the Environmental Services Department included the artwork as part of the grant—supported stormwater systems that were developed for the building. As a result of the grant, Brookner was able to create two environmental artworks at the building entrances that are visually striking, celebrate the capture of storm water from the roof, and slow its passage into Coyote Creek. The artworks, entitled "Urban Rain", take the form of two very different dynamic sculptures. The sculpture on the street side of the building is rectilinear and architectural in form, conducting water from a scupper through a transparent filtering system that is inscribed on its glass and steel surface with a map of San Jose's creeks. On the parking lot side, the water

is allowed to cascade freely from a scupper into a series of anthropomorphic, elevated chutes that direct the water into a pool covered with an dome inscribed with a pattern of pierced, spiraling slots. The backdrop for this sculpture is a mural painted by Scape Martinez that draws on the colors of the building and landscape and echoes the motion of the water cascading down the chutes.

Artists in our society are often at the forefront of social change, acting as predictors of trends and interpreters of new technologies. At Roosevelt Community Center, Jackie Brookner played this role, creating artworks that are both beautiful and illuminating. The artworks are an important addition to San Jose's Public Art collection and stand as an illustration of how art can make a difference in people's lives.

Barbara Goldstein

Barbara Goldstein is the Public Art Director for the City of San Jose Office of Cultural Affairs and the editor of *Public Art by the Book*, a primer recently published by Americans for the Arts and the University of Washington Press.

The City's Stormwater Program of the Environmental Services Department strives to engage the community to adopt practices that protect water quality by helping them understand the connection between our daily activities and the waterways we all share.

Many people understand that when the toilet flushes at home, that water and waste goes somewhere for treatment. What is far less understood is that the water that flows outdoors—rainwater or even irrigation water—flows across streets, lawns, roofs, parking lots, and sidewalks through the storm sewer system and into local creeks without treatment. And with that flow, come the pollutants from daily activities—yard trimmings and pesticides from gardening; oil, dirt, and cleaners from car washing; metal particulate from vehicles; litter from sidewalks and streets. And the list goes on. With sanitary sewage and large industrial facilities well served by treatment systems, the largest remaining contribution of pollution to our waterways, including the San Francisco Bay, is comprised of our daily choices. That can be both daunting and empowering. It means we can act as part of the solution.

In addition to working with the community to adopt eco-friendly practices, the City is also incorporating stormwater treatment into the built environment. Conventionally, when we build, we create more paved surfaces—more opportunity for rainfall runoff to carry pollutants and less opportunity for rainwater to infiltrate into the ground slowly and replenish our precious groundwater table. Spurred by water quality regulations, the City has in recent years begun requiring that development projects include features that treat stormwater runoff before that water enters the storm sewer system. These features can be natural systems that look like landscape or mechanical devices—both are designed to trap or filter pollutants and hold water before release. The best designs seek to restore or mimic the way water moved before the building, with slow release and infiltration of rainwater.

In 2005, funding from the Stormwater Program was set aside for stormwater treatment demonstration projects. The purpose was to install treatment features into public projects to demonstrate how these features function. Just as we were evaluating opportunities for a suitable location, an unexpected opportunity arose. The City's Public Art Program approached the Stormwater team to collaborate on the public art for Roosevelt Community Center. The artist for the project, Jackie Brookner, thought the Center's location adjacent to Coyote Creek made it ideal for highlighting the interface between the urban landscape and natural systems.

Brookner drew upon the expertise of City staff from the fields of engineering, biology, environmental education and graphic design and created an inspired set of artworks for Roosevelt Community Center that reveal and celebrate the journey of rainwater through the urban environment to local creeks. Rainfall from the roof flows to two featured works of art, which on their own are beautiful and evocative of the natural environment. What is magical is they are also functioning to treat the stormwater.

There are significant environmental benefits from this project. First, the stormwater system, integrated into the artwork, will reduce the volume and improve the quality of the water entering the storm sewer system, Coyote Creek, and ultimately the San Francisco Bay. Second, by providing demonstrations and monitoring, the artwork will expose and encourage these approaches to our community of developers and residents.

For the Stormwater team, the original goal was to showcase stormwater treatment measures. What emerged was a design that featured stormwater treatment as truly integrated into the design, both form and function, for the building. The design swiftly exceeds all expectation as it conveys through art work literally and figuratively the not often seen story of how rainwater connects us all to our creeks, rivers, and oceans. The artwork will raise public awareness of stormwater and the importance of a healthy watershed, fostering stewardship within the adjacent communities and for all visitors.

Melody Tovar
Melody Tovar is Deputy Director of Watershed Protection
City of San Jose Environmental Services

The Roosevelt Community Center was conceived as a place that welcomes, reflects and energizes the community through a broad range of activities and an open spirit of social interaction and education. The building celebrates the community's support for a sustainable society through the full integration and clear expression of energy-conserving and environmentally-friendly materials, systems and architectural strategies.

From the very beginning, the City of San Jose, the community, and designers Group 4 Architecture, Research + Planning embraced a holistic approach to creating a sustainable new Roosevelt Community Center, starting with the location of the new building on previously developed property next to Roosevelt Park in order to preserve open space. Siting the building on the street weaves it into the urban fabric while creating a gateway to the park beyond.

Careful building massing and solar orientation bring sunlight deep into the building, minimizing the need for artificial lighting during the day. Interior lights in public areas are sensor-controlled, automatically dimming or shutting off in response to available daylight and room occupancy. A heavily-insulated exterior building envelope, roof overhangs and exterior sunshades protect interior spaces from the sun's heat. As a result, the Roosevelt Community Center outperforms California energy standards by more than 40%.

Throughout the community center, durable materials were used that will not require frequent maintenance or replacement. Wood used in the building is from certified sustainable forests. Where possible, materials were sourced from local manufacturers to reduce the environmental impacts of long-distance transportation. Interior materials and finishes have high recycled content and low levels of volatile organic compounds (VOCs). Much of the waste and debris generated during construction was diverted from landfills to local recycling facilities.

Water quality and conservation are major contributors to the building's reduced environmental footprint. Dual-flush toilets, low-flow urinals, and metered faucets with automatic sensors save significant amounts of water compared to standard fixtures. Irrigation of landscaping and the park is carefully controlled and uses reclaimed water.

The important role that sustainably-designed buildings can play in protecting the environment is highlighted at Roosevelt Community Center in ecological art pieces that also take an active role in the building's stormwater management system. The Coyote Creek Filter highlights how the design protects water quality in Coyote Creek and the San Francisco Bay, exposing the rainwater treatment process by collecting runoff from the roof and filtering it through layers of rock. The Thumbprint Filter also collects, filters, and detains rainwater from the roof, diverting it into site bioswales. Bioswales and infiltration basins reduce demand on the city's stormwater system and improve the quality of water entering Coyote Creek by extracting pollutants and debris from rainwater and allowing it to percolate into the soil to recharge the local aquifer.

One objective measure of the community center's sustainability is its participation in the Leadership in Energy and Environmental Design (LEED) program, a nationally-accepted objective benchmark for the design, construction and operation of high performance green buildings. LEED projects can receive Certified, Silver, Gold, or even Platinum ratings based on the types and extent of strategies incorporated. The Roosevelt Community Center targets certification at the Gold level, the highest of any City of San Jose project to date.

At the heart of the Roosevelt Community Center's success is its whole-building approach to sustainable design, capitalizing on natural and passive processes that minimize the project's impact on the environment. The community center's high level of environmental leadership forms a strong foundation and inspiration for the community as it continues to create and embrace a sustainable future.

Jonathan Hartman
Jonathan Hartman, LEEDap, is the Project Architect for the Roosevelt Community Center and an Associate at the San Francisco Bay Area firm Group 4 Architecture, Research + Planning, Inc.

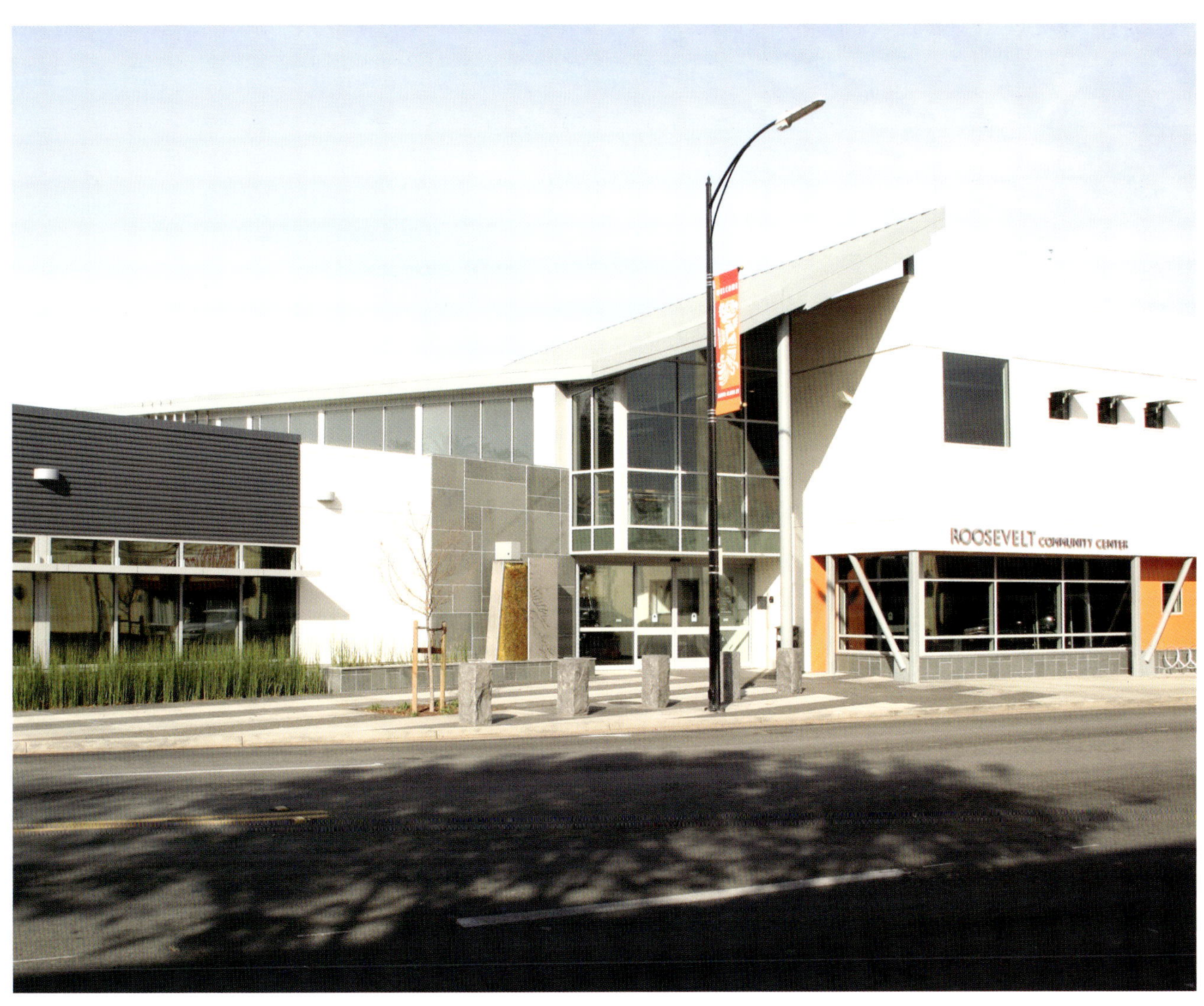

URBAN RAIN

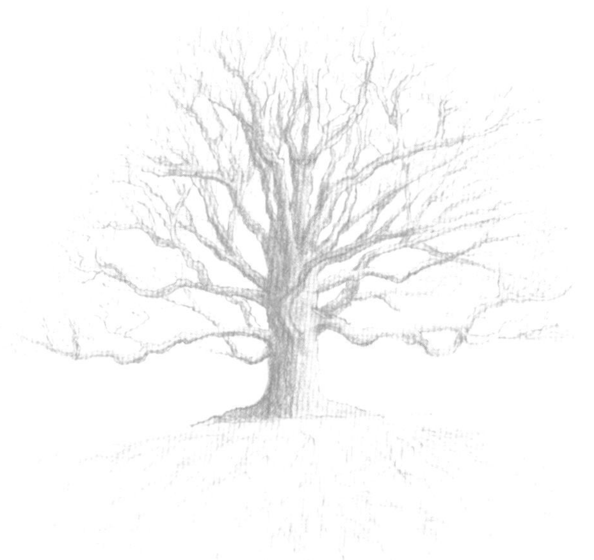

Whenever in this city we see rain, we see ourselves. Whenever we experience water in any form—whether as cloud, lake, stream, mist, ocean, ice, rainbow, flood, snow or swamp—we experience ourselves let loose. Our hearts echo the pulsing of ocean waves, while the fluids of our blood are exactly as salty as ocean water. Each one of us and each one of the billions of cells in our bodies is at least 70% water. In fact all living organisms are mostly water. Spiral forms, meanders and branching patterns reveal water's hidden presence in our bodies and throughout nature, and like family crests remind us of our lineage and kinship.

When I first learned I would have the opportunity to create work for the new Roosevelt Community Center, obvious questions came to mind. Who is "the community" the new center will serve, what age groups, what ethnic backgrounds? What is the context of the building in relation to surrounding neighborhoods and the park? Like pebbles thrown into a pond, these first questions rippled outward as more basic questions emerged. What is a community center? What does the idea of community imply? Are there aspects of "community" that are hidden?

While each of us might identify with a particular community we really belong to many coexisting and overlapping communities. Nested one within another, family, friends, neighborhood, generation, work, school, religious group, ethnic group, city, nation (not to mention our various political, sports, and fashion affiliations) shape who we think we are and how we identify ourselves.

Any community is defined by who belongs to it, but it is defined just as much by who does not belong, the "them" outside its edges. Within the fiction of "them" are the unseen and too often unacknowledged supports of our lives. Close in there are the people who pick up the garbage, or sweep the streets, and further away in our global culture—those who plant the food we eat, make our cars or sew the clothes we wear.

The true extended family of community is even larger. The vitality of any community and the continuity of its cultural heritage depend upon the health of the natural world that sustains it. "The community" really includes all the natural systems and other species that support our human lives. Here at Roosevelt Community Center this means the rain that falls on the ground and is stored in it—the water that will feed the rivers and satisfy our thirst. It also means the air we breathe, and the trees and plants that give us oxygen and food. It means the insects that pollinate the trees and plants, and the sun that gives the trees the energy they need to grow and that gives us warmth. And we can't forget the billions of bacteria that live in our gut to help us digest our food. We quite literally are the water and earth and air and fire our bodies take in. Being alive means being part of this community.

When rain falls in natural environments, the leaves of trees slow its fall. The rainwater gradually penetrates into the soil and is stored underground where it can remain, be drawn up by plant and tree roots or slowly make its way to become part of nearby rivers and streams. The hard surfaces of cities with their paving and buildings prevent this infiltration process.

Rainfall in the city runs very quickly across the hard surfaces of roofs, streets, parking lots and sidewalks, picking up various pollutants along the way, from oil and grease to heavy metals and animal droppings. It then enters the nearest waterways, bringing all these pollutants with it, destroying the delicate chemical balance of the water to cause overpopulation of some organisms while killing off others. At Roosevelt Community Center, the nearest waterway is Coyote Creek.

"If you could tell people one thing about water, what would it be?" I asked James Downing, the City Biologist, who was my guide along Coyote Creek. He said, *"Any time people touch water, they touch the streams and oceans."* To keep pollutants from entering the rivers, we need to respect stormwater as the precious resource that it is, rather than seeing it as waste and trying to get rid of it as fast as possible. We need to slow down its journey keeping the rain near where it falls so it can soak into the ground to let the soil and soil microbes filter out any pollutants.

My work at Roosevelt Community Center tells some of the story of how the building itself and everyone who uses it touch the surrounding waters. **Urban Rain** consists of two sculpture installations at the South and North entrances of the building that collect and filter stormwater runoff from the roof. **The Coyote Creek Filter** and **The Thumbprint Filter** celebrate what is often undervalued as waste, reveal processes that are usually invisible and create innovative methods for dealing with stormwater runoff from the building to help protect Coyote Creek.

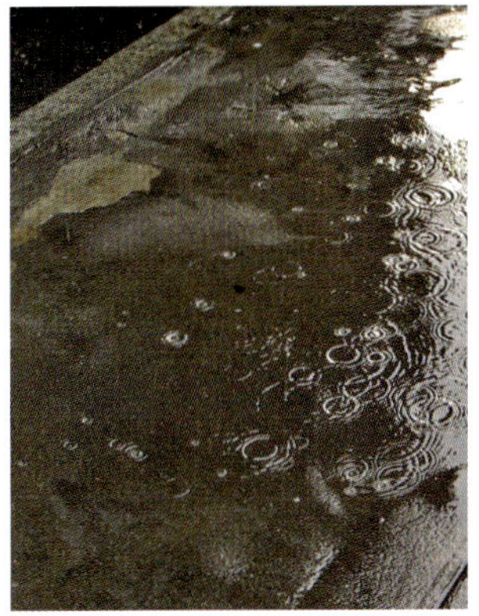

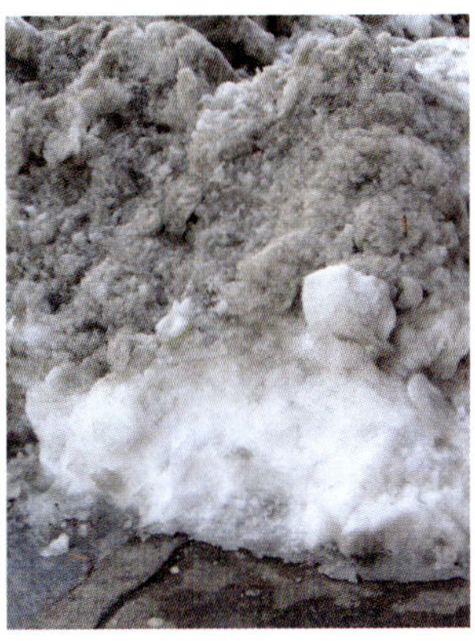

The invisible pollutants in stormwater runoff become visible with day old city snow.

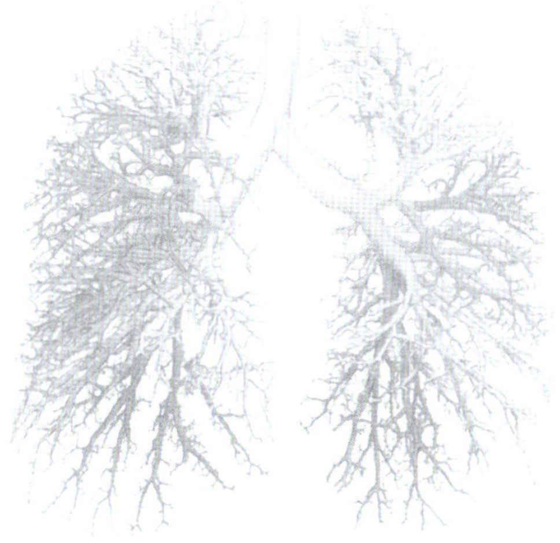

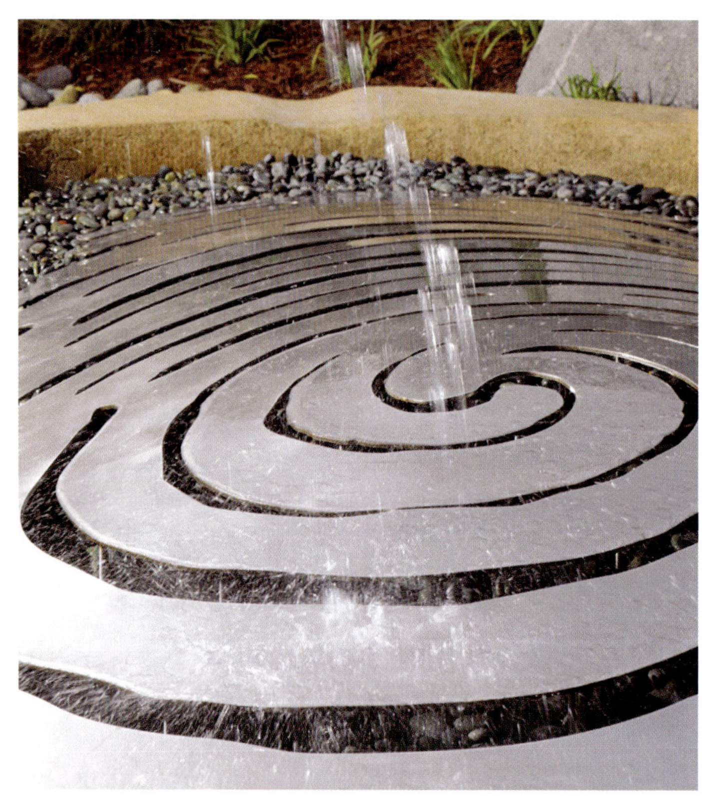

The rivers engrave our palms, the galaxies our fingertips. JACKIE BROOKNER

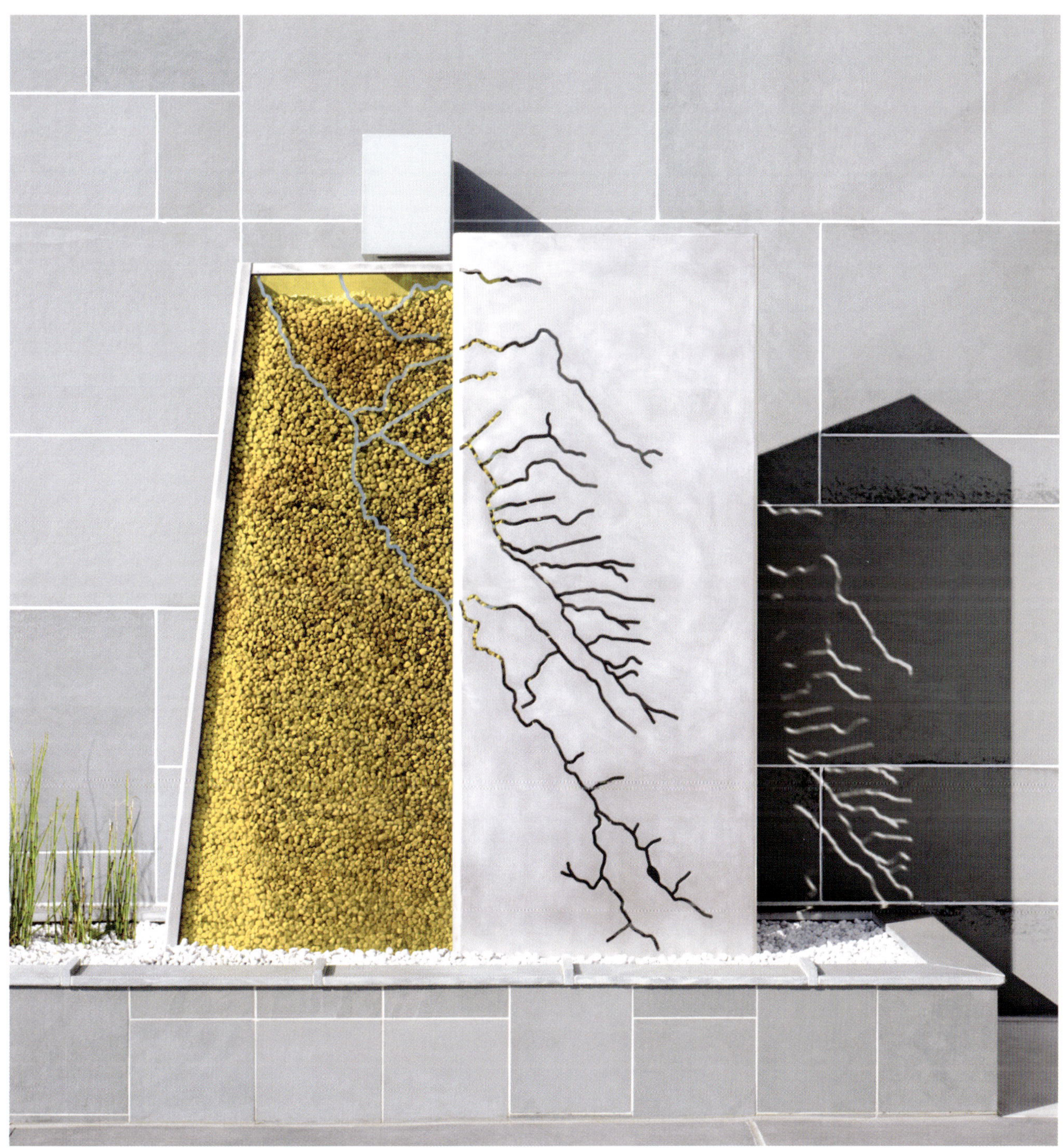

THE PROJECT

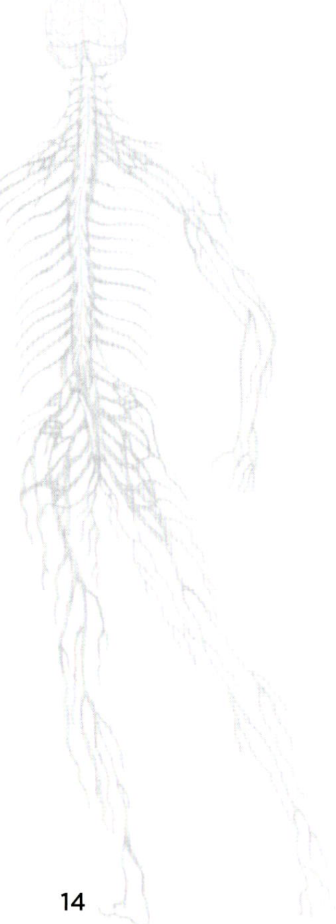

The Coyote Creek Filter at the South Entry to the building celebrates water and the infiltration process. Water coming from the roof passes through the scupper box above the glass filter. The rocks inside slow down the flow of the water and filter it (with the help of microorganisms that live in the spaces between the rocks). Usually we cannot see this process because it happens underground in the soil.

The vein-like image that is etched into the glass and continues across the stainless steel panel next to the glass is a map of the paths that Coyote Creek and all its tributaries follow to eventually empty into San Francisco Bay. All of the land area drained by this stream system makes up Coyote Creek's watershed. The idea of a watershed is very abstract and hard to picture. This is because we cannot see watersheds and because they connect things we think of as quite separate and different. They connect kitchen sinks with clouds in the sky, rooftops with fish in the river, mountain streams with urban streets, and automobiles with the bay. The watershed map on the *Coyote Creek Filter* also connects things that are separate and different.

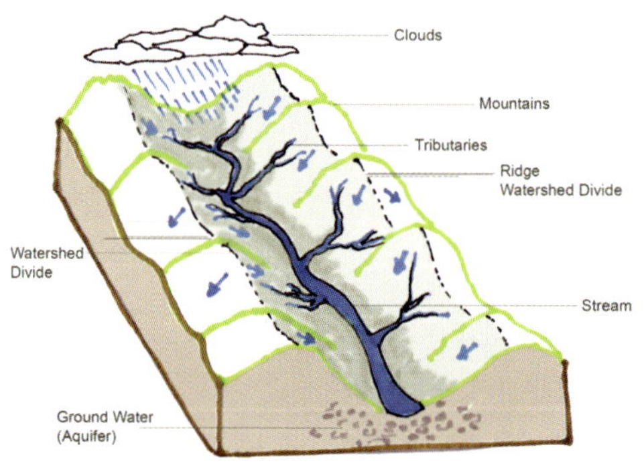

A Watershed

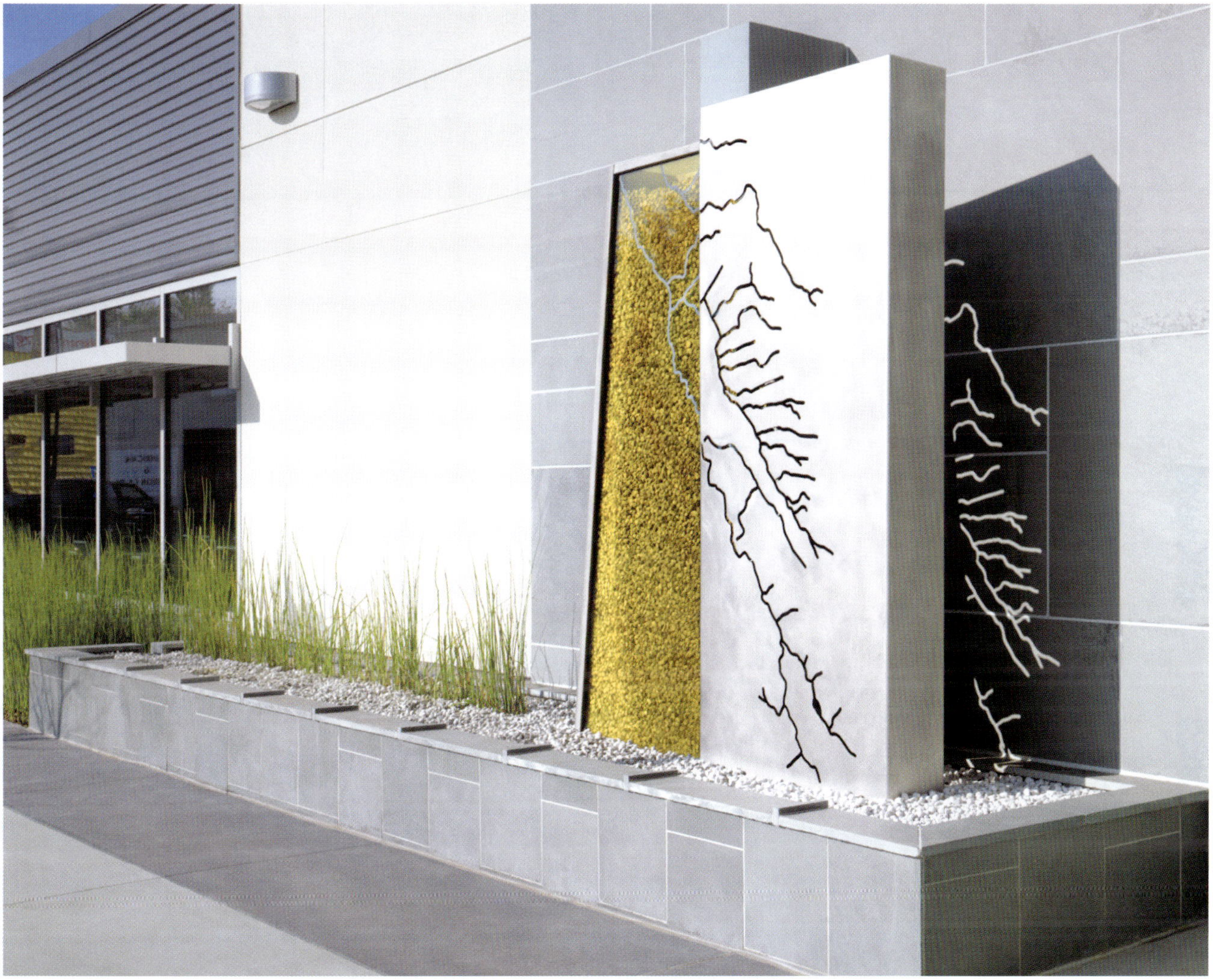

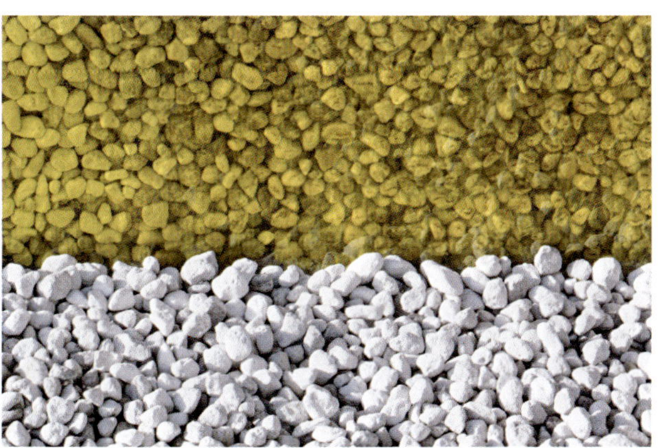

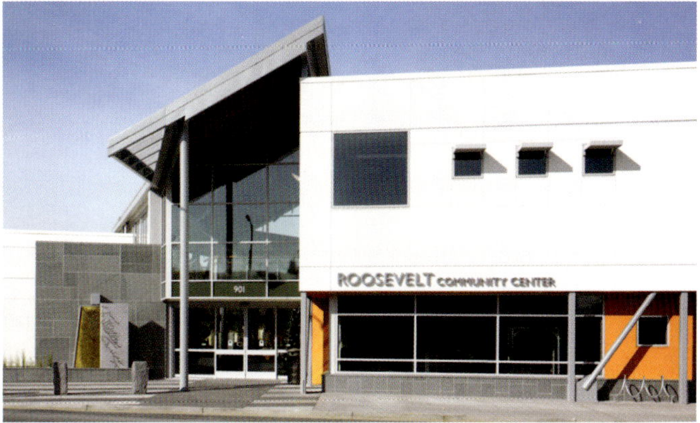
901
ROOSEVELT COMMUNITY CENTER

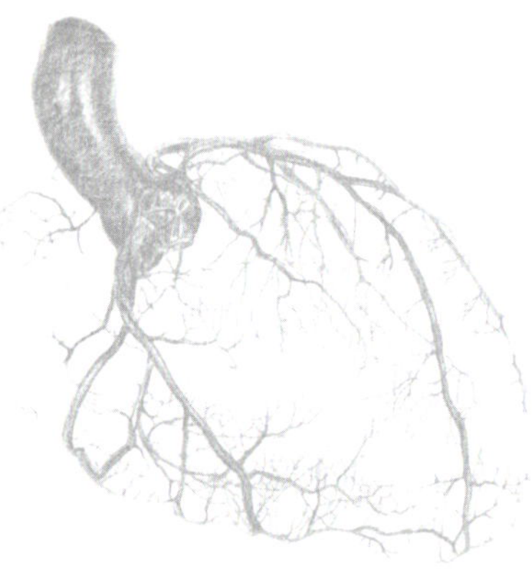

Facing page

The Coyote Creek watershed panel is illuminated from behind at night, highlighting the watershed map.

Right

The *Coyote Creek Filter* seen from the second floor window shows the glass and steel container filled with white pumice and the scupper box above it.

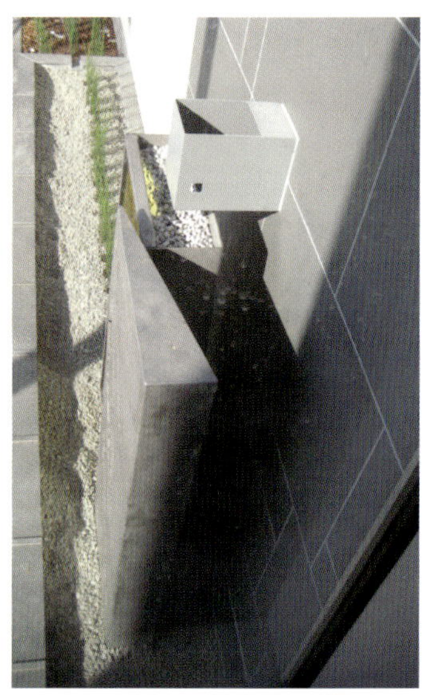

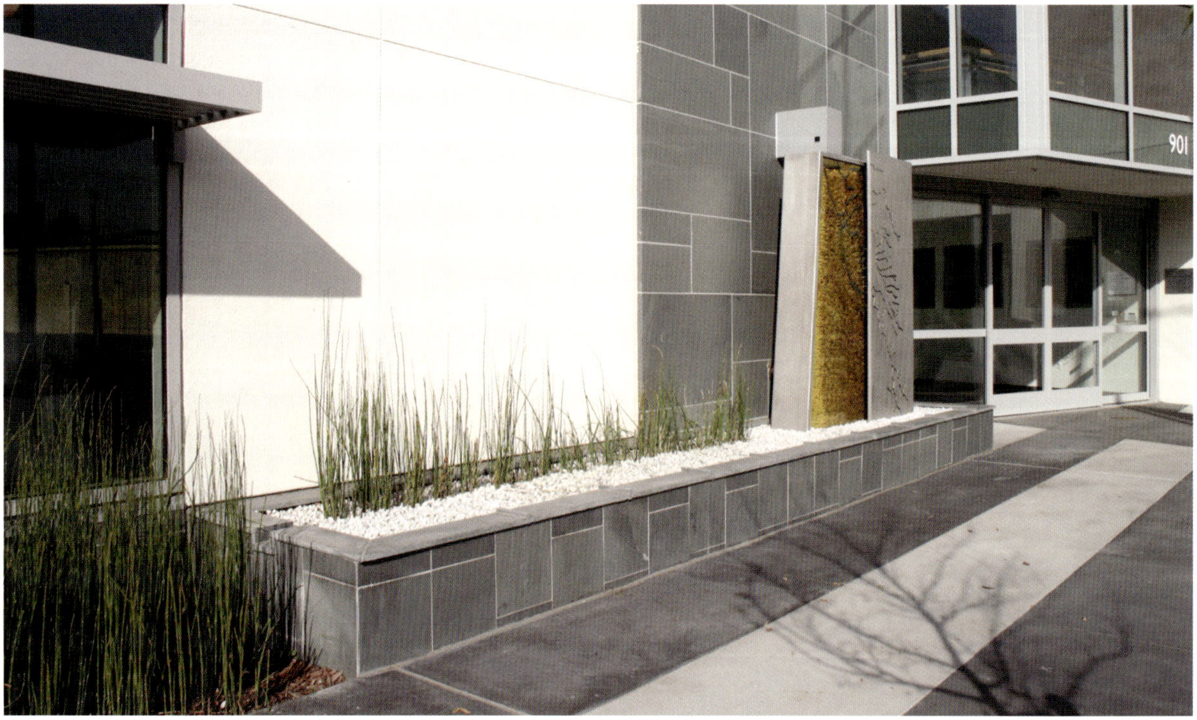

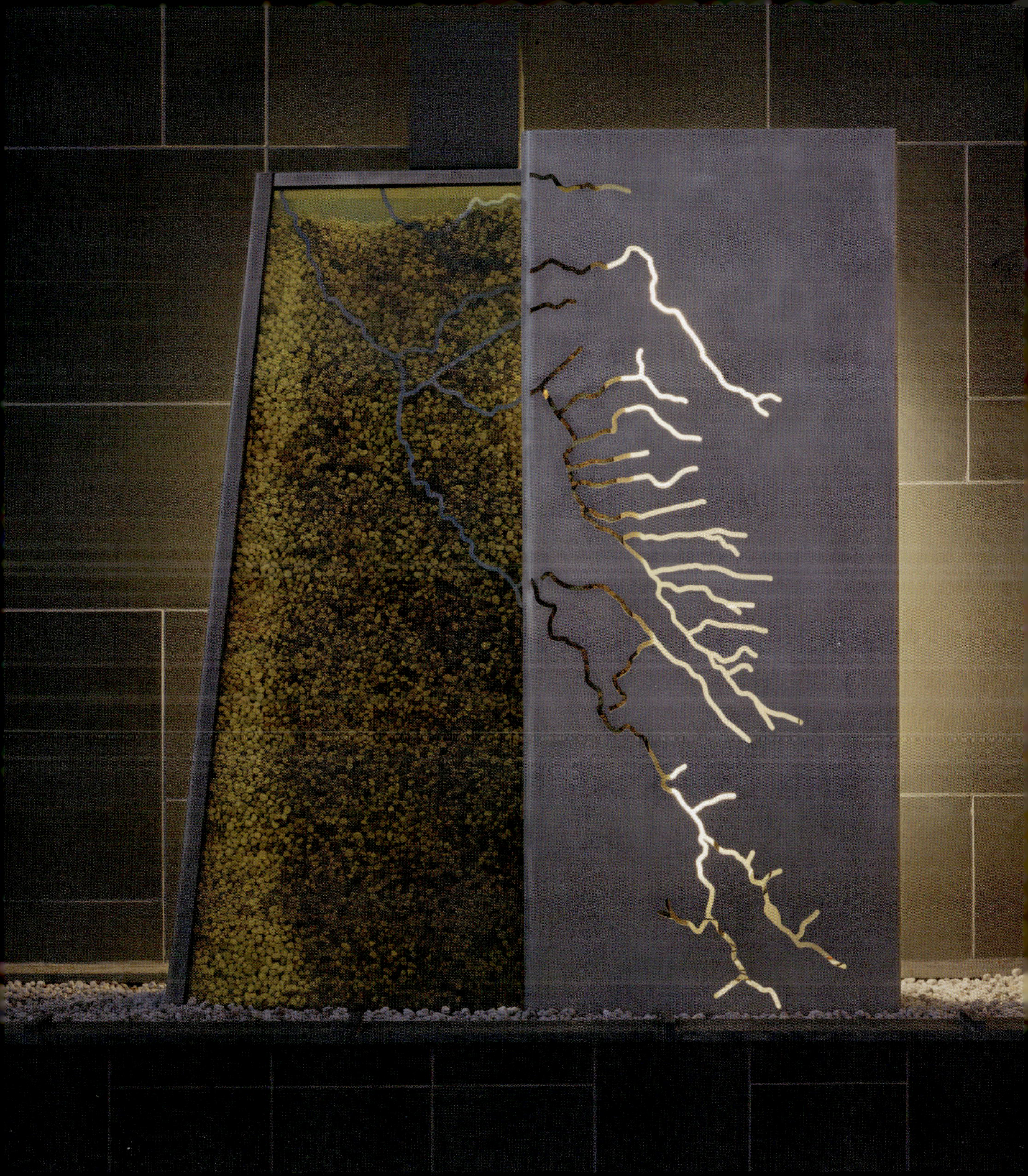

Chutes and Thumbprint Filter
Stainless steel, concrete, filter rock
Chutes: 16 x 13 x 6'
Seating wall: 21' x 13' x 20"
Background mural: Edward (Scape) Martinez

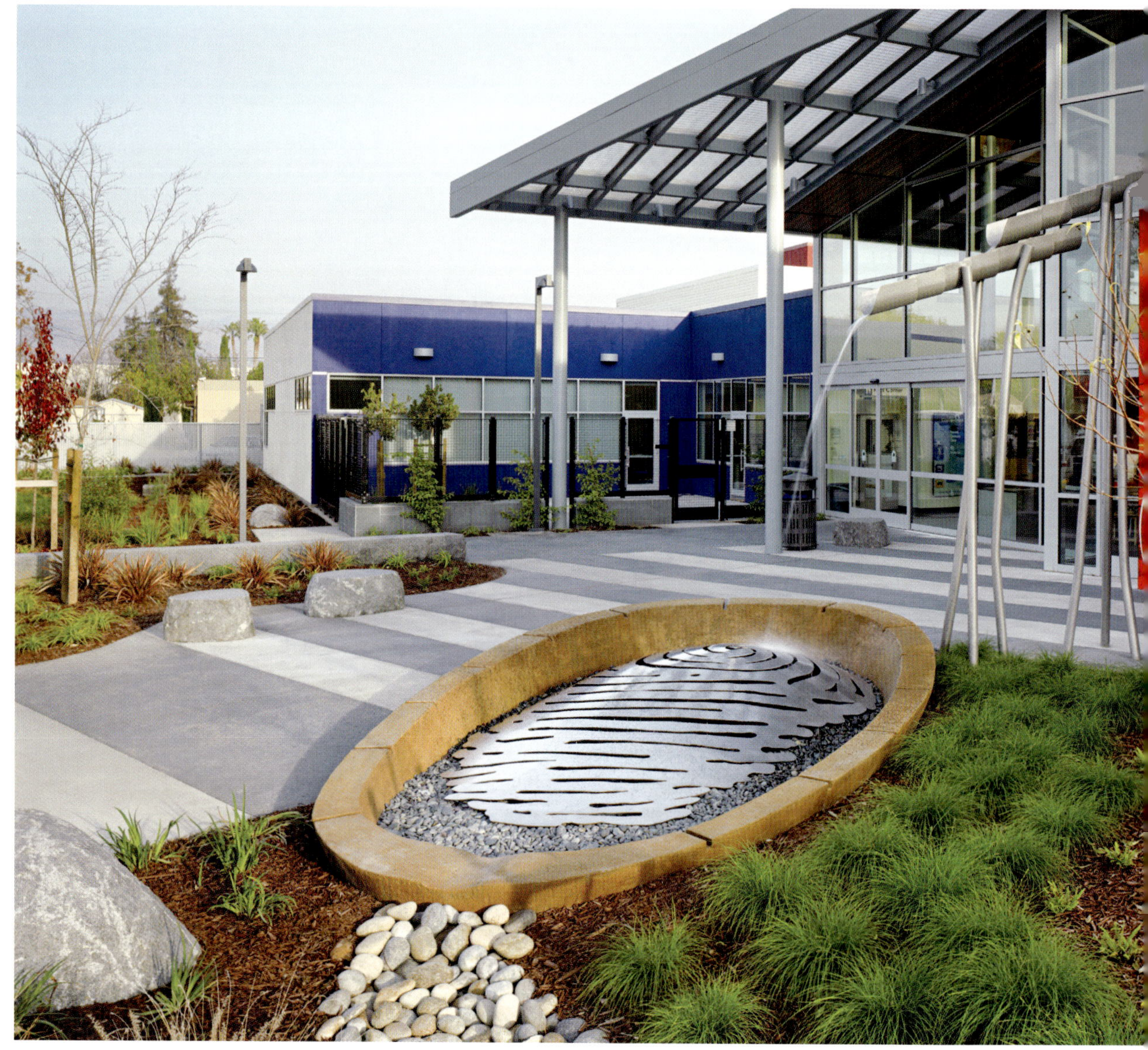

Whenever people touch water, they touch the streams and oceans. JAMES DOWNING

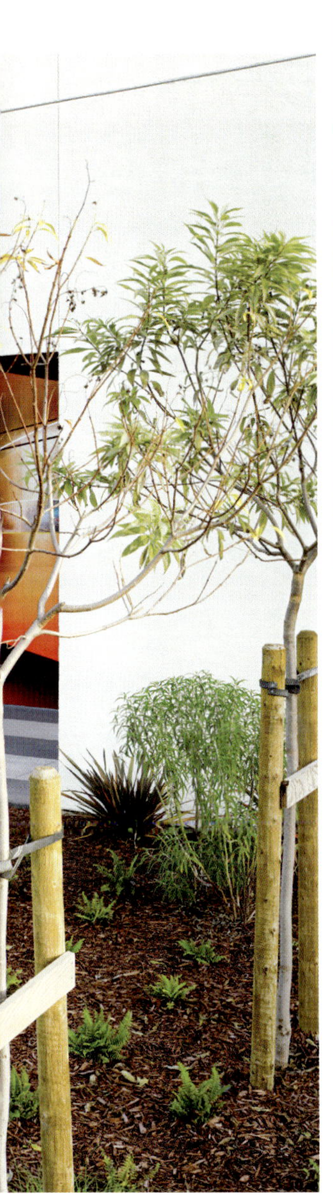

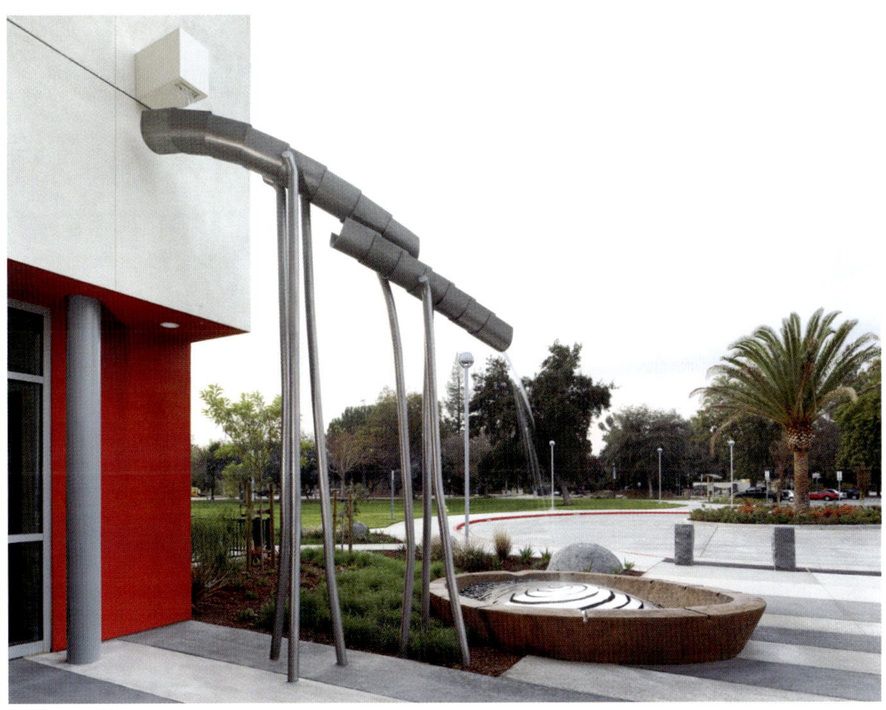

At the North entry are the Chutes and Thumbprint Filter. Rainwater from the roof passes through the scupper box at the corner of the building. The water travels down the water chutes and drops onto the Thumbprint in the filter pool below where it is detained and filtered by the rocks before it flows out into the bioswale.

The spiral pattern of the stainless steel sculpture is based on a real thumbprint. The whorls of our fingerprints echo the spiral eddies of water, wind and galaxies. Our fingerprints reveal both our unique individuality and our common origin in the universe.

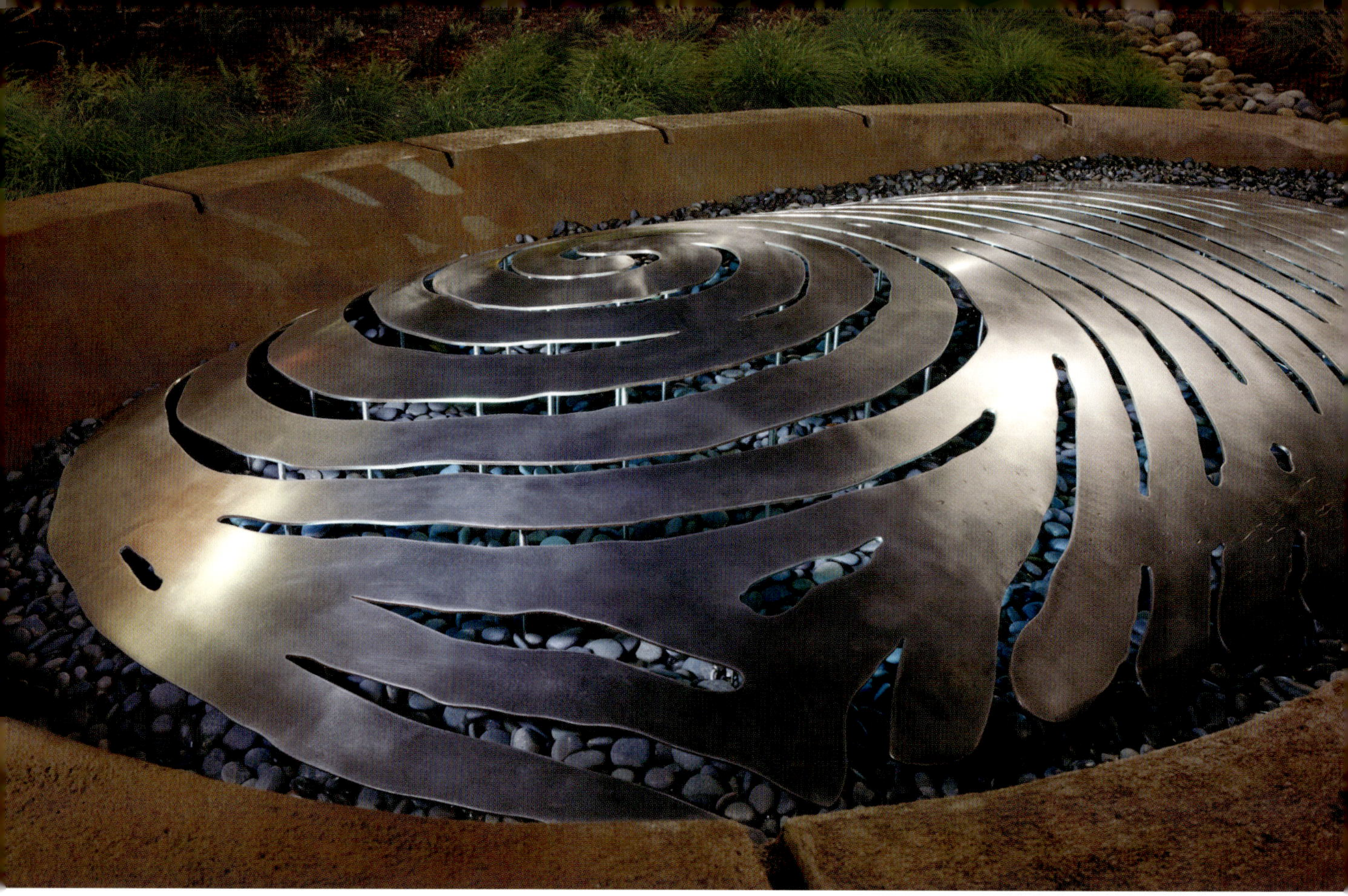

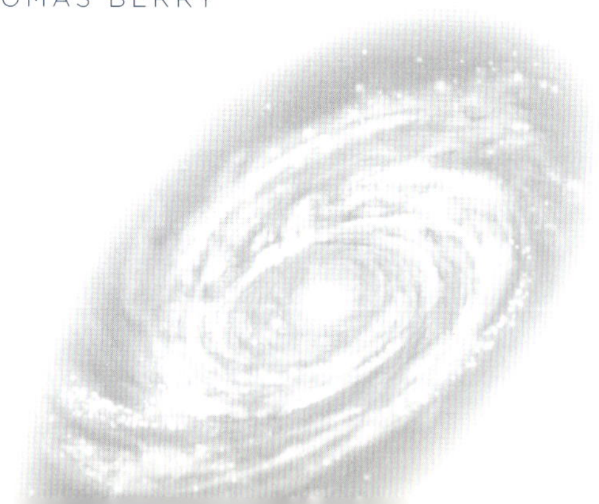

We bear the universe in our being as the universe bears us in its being. THOMAS BERRY

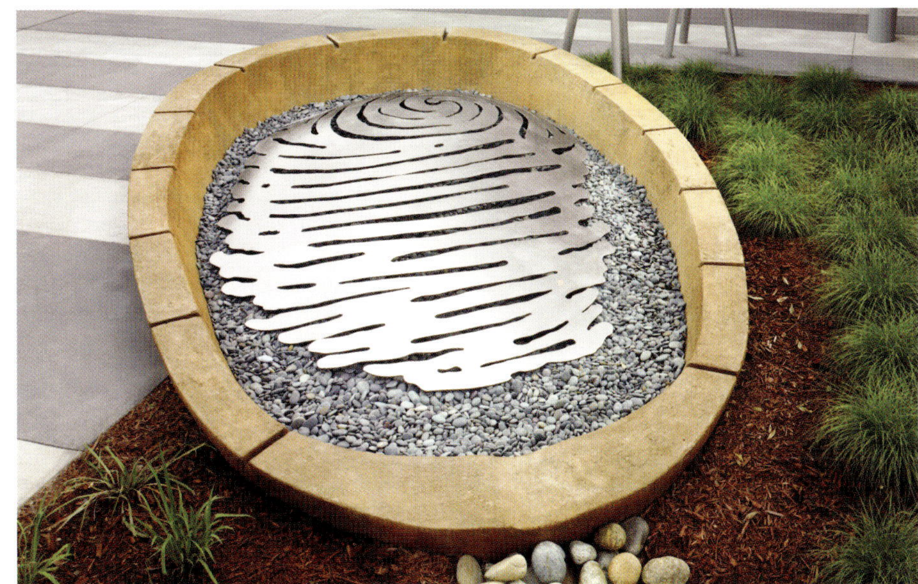

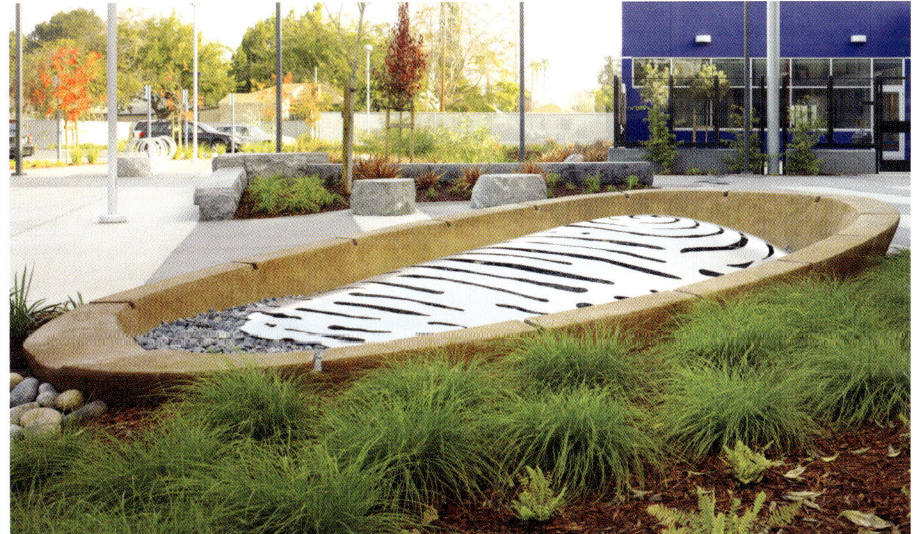

Left

The Thumbprint Filter is illuminated from below at night.

Right

The concrete seating wall is the container for a layer of filtration rocks two feet deep. The volume is large enough to detain and filter runoff from 5700 sq. ft. of roof area for a .5 inch storm.

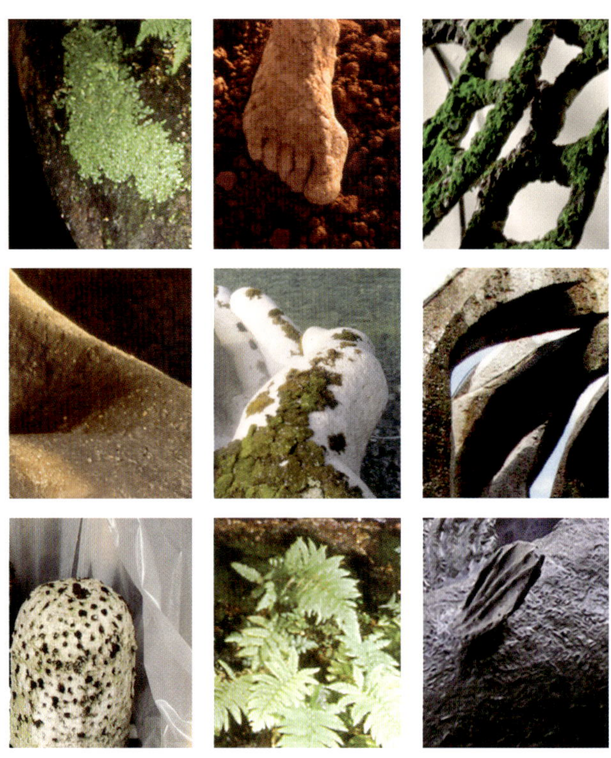

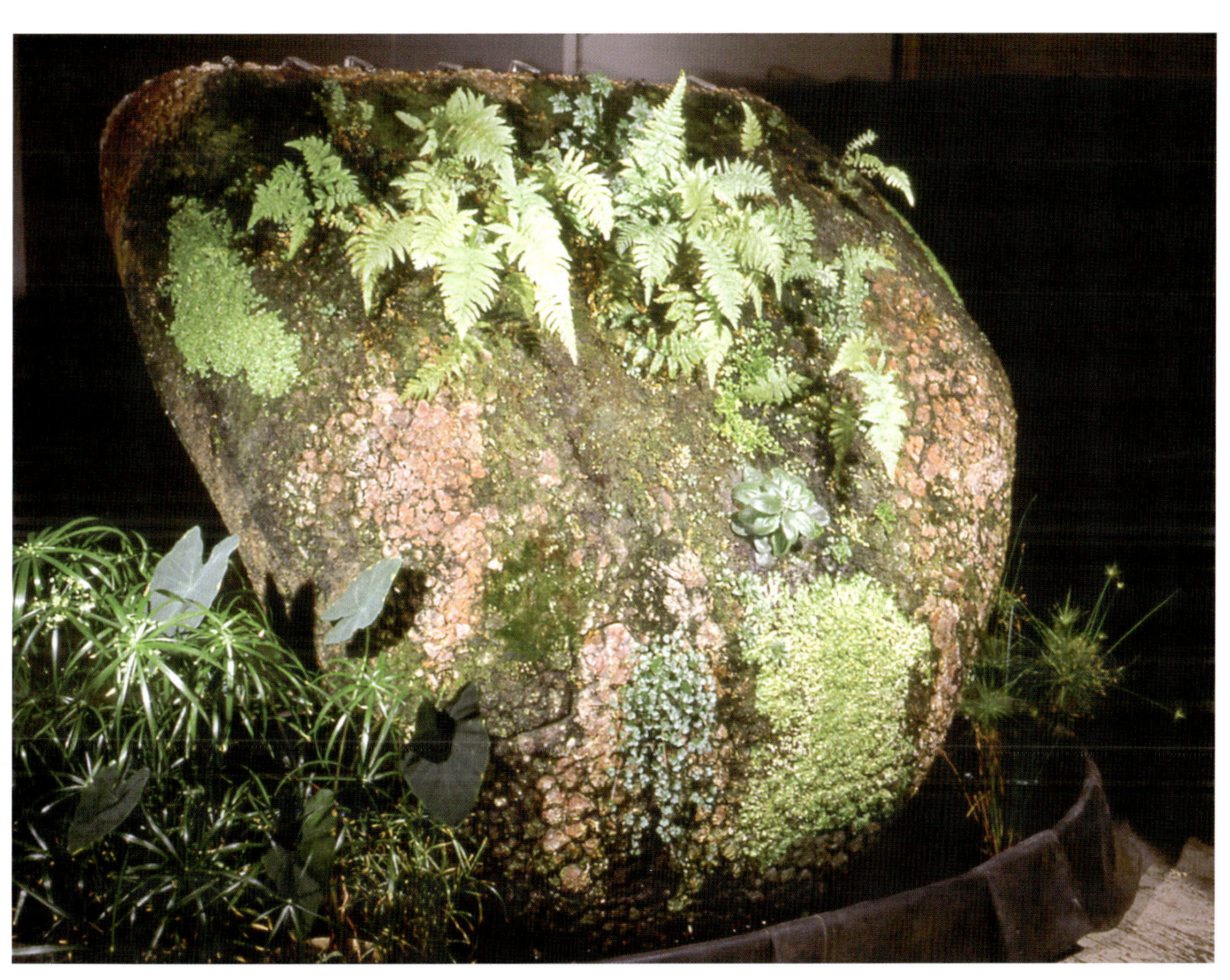

ROOTS OF AN ECOLOGICAL ART

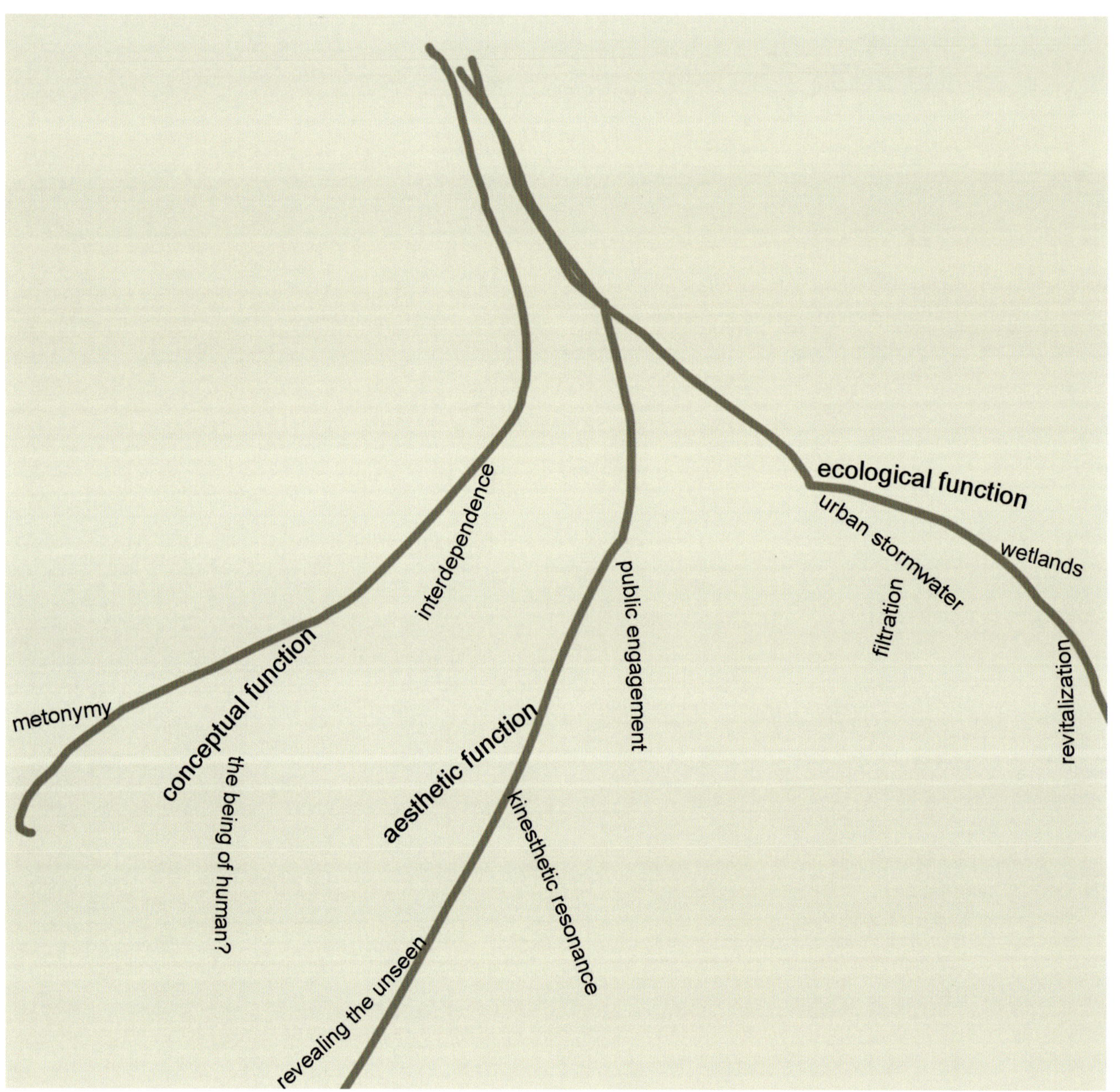

Three levels of function form the roots of my work.

Most of my works focus on water remediation. Whenever the climate allows, I create sculpted ecosystems I call Biosculptures™ that use the capacity of carefully chosen plants to clean and filter water. Made of mosses, ferns and other plants growing on stone and concrete structures, they provide ecological and aesthetic solutions to water quality (what's in the water) and water quantity (how much water) problems for parks, wetlands, stormwater runoff, and greywater. Biosculptures™ demonstrate that there is no waste in healthy natural systems. Instead, the plants and the bacteria living in their root zones transform the pollutants and toxins in the water flowing over them into life sustaining nutrients. The "waste" from the fish, snails, and other aquatic organisms living in the water becomes food for the plants.

Prima Lingua
1995-present
64 x 101 x 80"
(First Tongue/
First Language).
This monstrously
large tongue that
licks the polluted
water it stands in
is my prototype
Biosculpture™ and an
ongoing test piece.

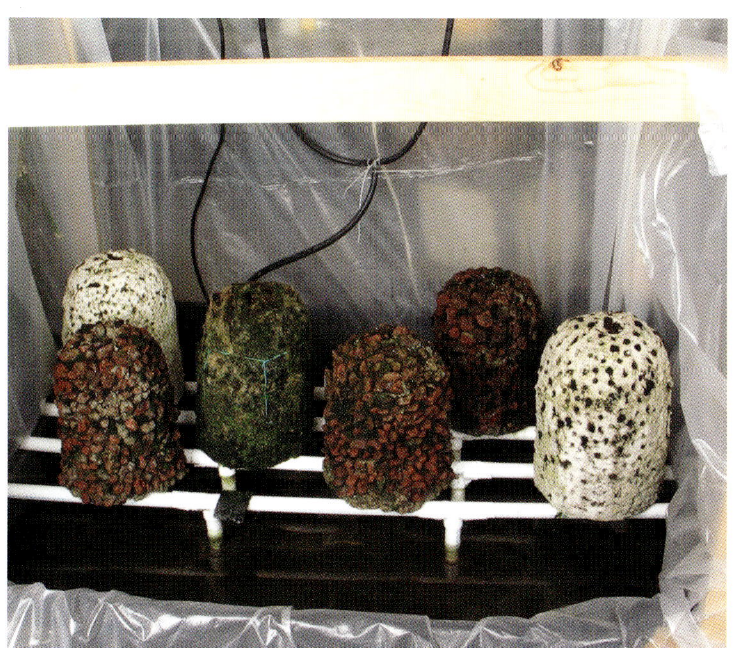

Cornell Tests
2005
13 x 8 x 8" each
These small
sculptures were made
for Environmental
Engineering research
at Cornell University.
The experimental
results demonstrated
their capacity to
remove high levels of
common stormwater
pollutants (including
lead, phosphorus,
copper, cadmium
and zinc) at two
levels of acidity (pH
2.5 and 6.5).

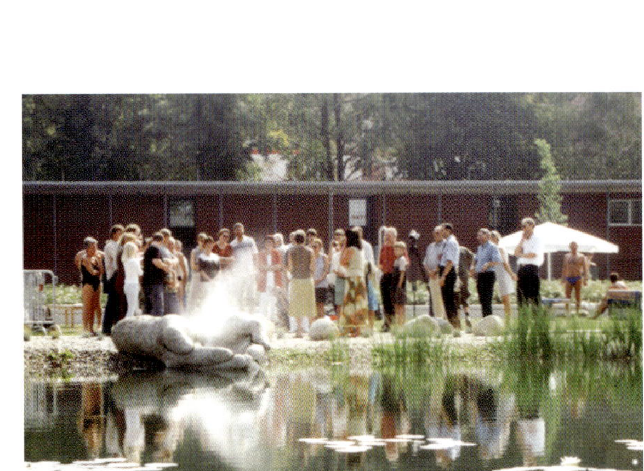

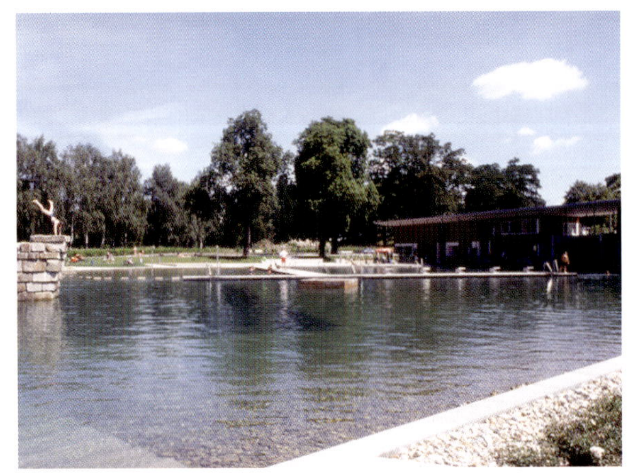

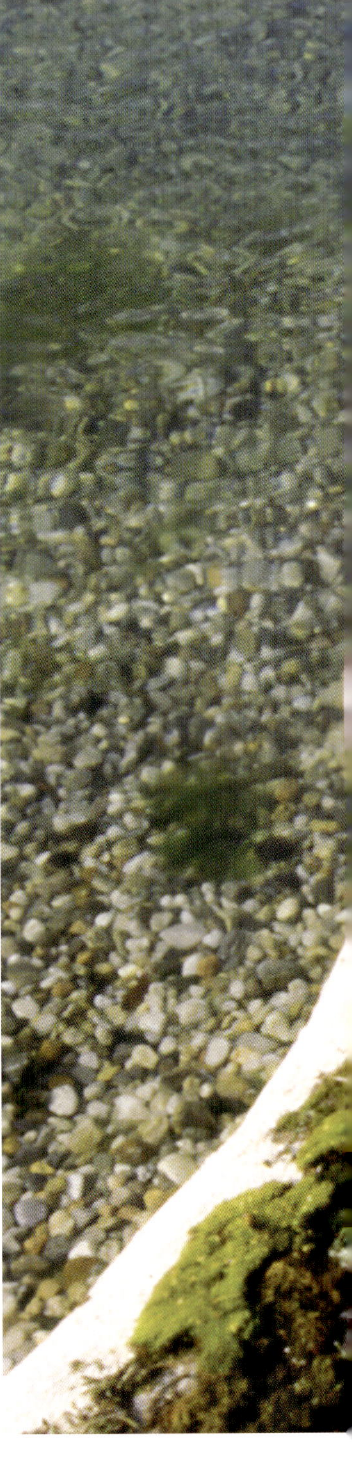

The Gift of Water
2001
3 x 5 x 9'
This Biosculpture™ in Grossenhain, near Dresden, Germany is part of a remarkable public swimming complex that is used by over 1500 people a day. The water is filtered entirely by plants in a constructed wetland, without the use of chlorine or any other chemicals. Two cupped hand, overgrown with mosses, reach from the bank into the pond. Water flowing into the hands mists the mosses which in turn purify the water.

26

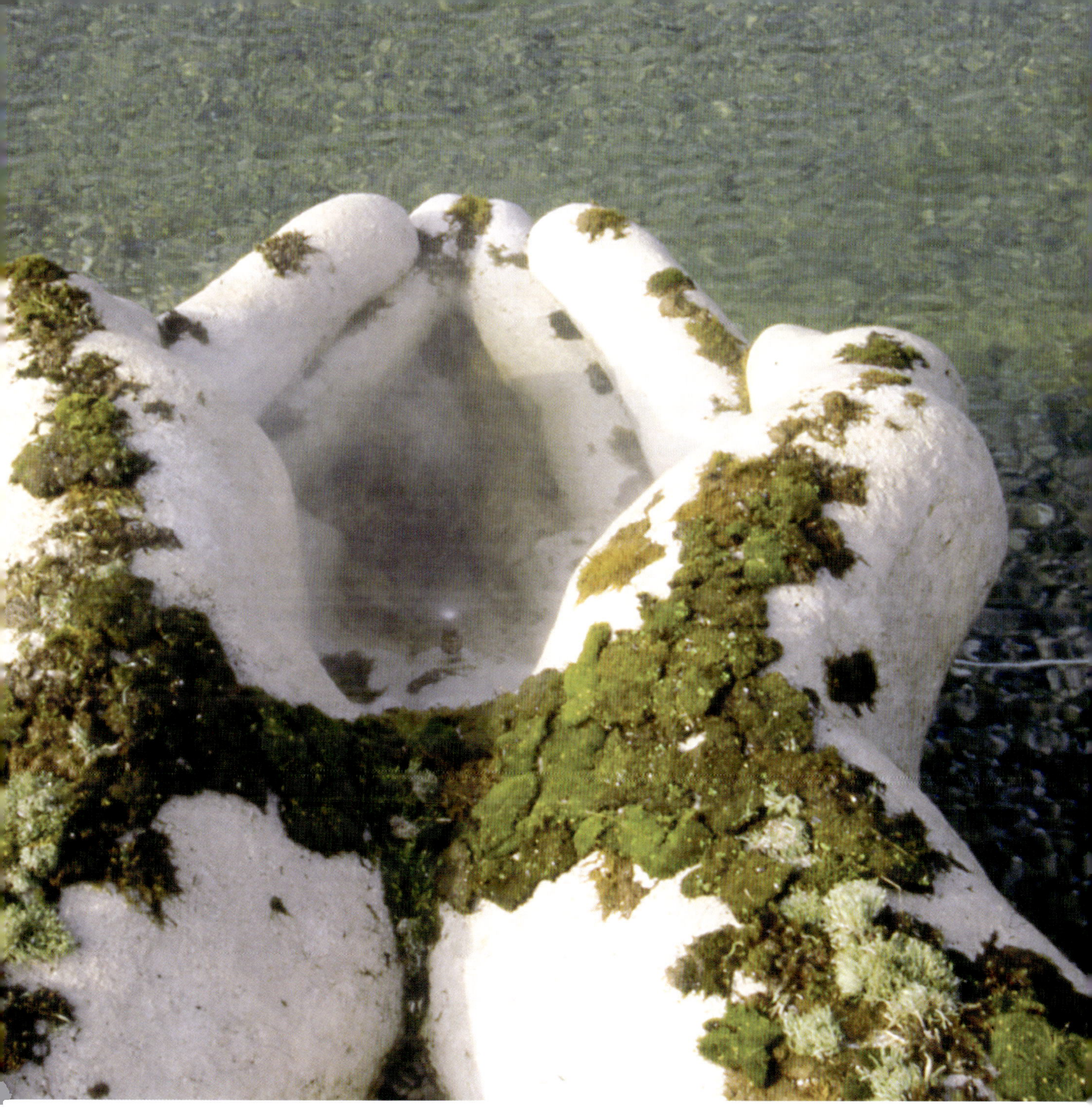

Tongue Lounge
1993
44 x 60 x 36"

Rocking Tongue
1995
41 x 59 x 26"

Two of a series of
tongue chairs in
which I wanted
people to feel
embraced by soil.
They ask to be
experienced with
the whole body.

Of Earth and Cotton
Upper right:
Detail of installation
McKissick Museum
Columbia, SC
1994
Lower right:
Installation at
University of North
Texas, Denton, TX
1995
18" x 50 x 40'

These are portraits
of the feet of people
who picked and
farmed cotton by
hand in the 1930s and
40s. The exhibition
evolved as it traveled
across the Southern
United States from
1994-8 following the
migration of cotton
farming.

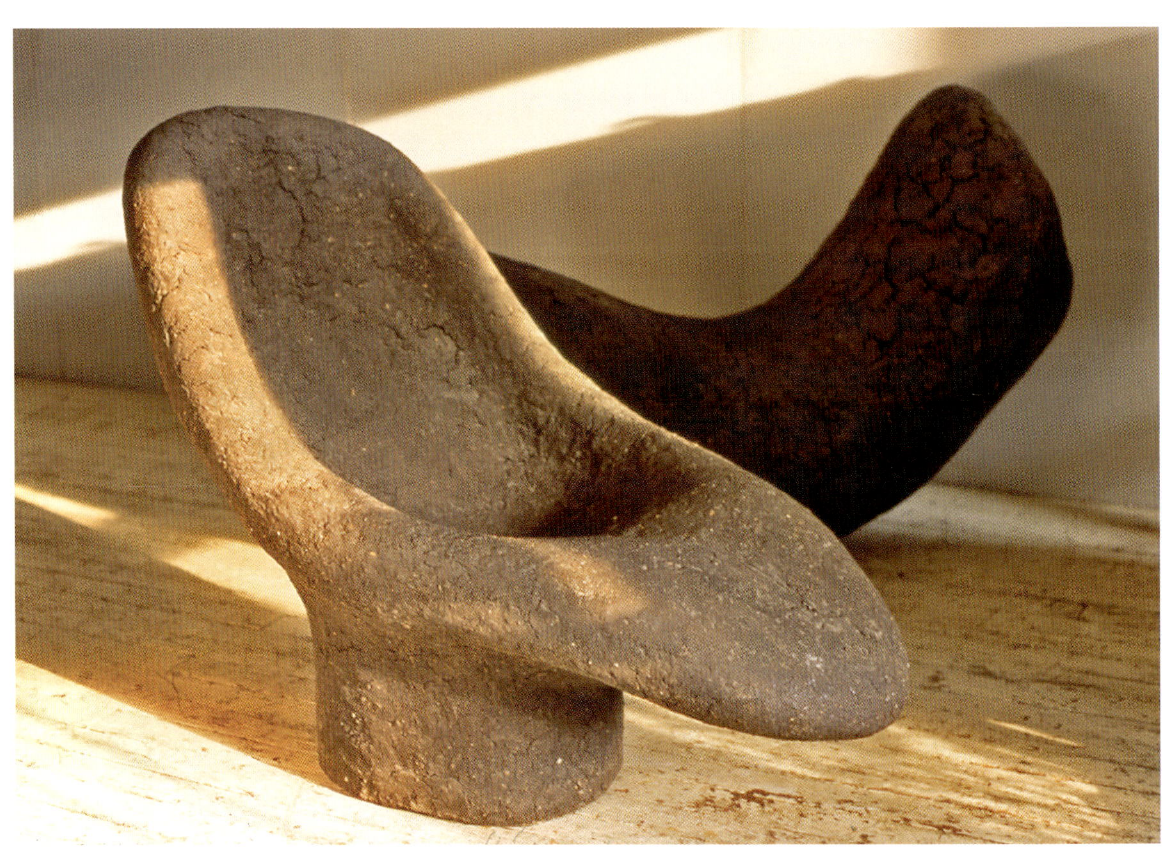

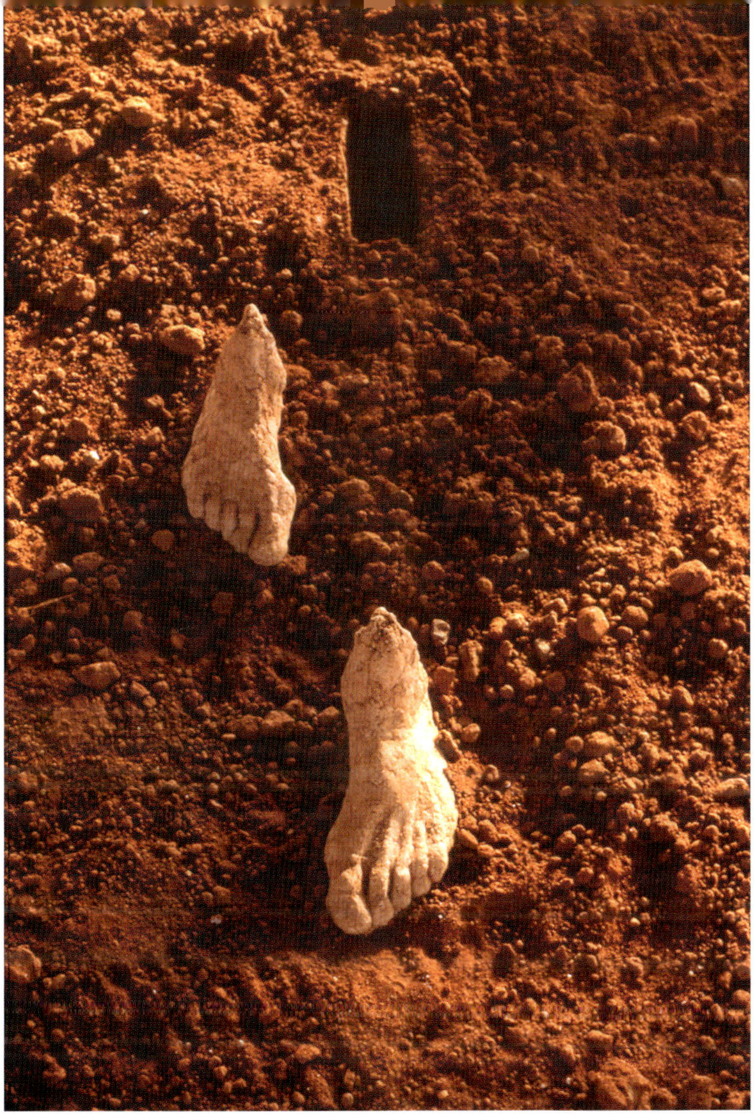

For many years, I have found myself using a part of the body to stand for the whole (a figure of speech called metonymy)—with the feet in *Of Earth and Cotton*, the tongues of the dirt chairs and *Prima Lingua*, the hands in *The Gift of Water*, and now with the *Thumbprint Filter*. I finally understood why I was doing this while I was making *The Gift of Water*. These hands, cut off at the wrists, are parts of the body that feel like a whole yet insistently declare themselves as parts. This reflects a truth about our bodies. The experience we have of our bodies as a contained whole is only partly true. It ignores the fact and nature's demand that to continue to exist we must be open—exchanging with the world around us, taking in and letting go.

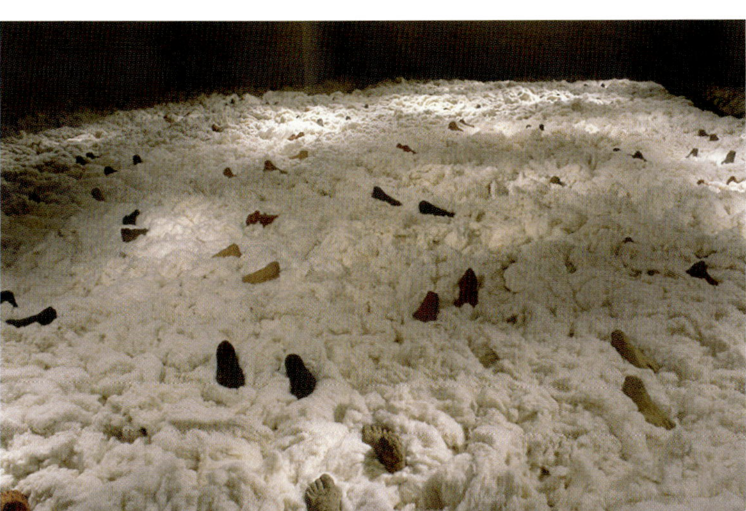

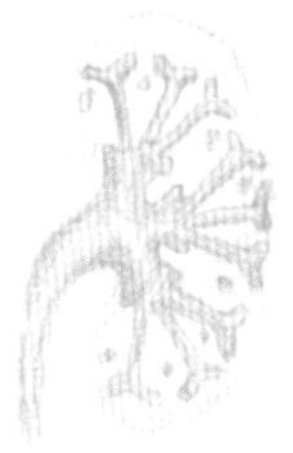

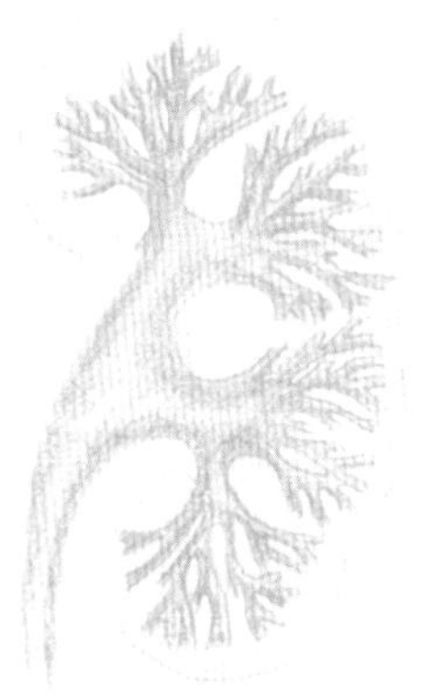

The continuity of patterning throughout nature provides structural evidence for the common origin and interdependence of all of earth's inhabitants and natural systems. The branching or dendritic patterns (from the Latin word *dendros*, meaning tree or branches) we see in river systems, trees, and leaves occur throughout our bodies in our veins, lungs, nervous system, and even on our palms.

Facing page

I'm You
Installation at Wave Hill, Bronx, NY
2000
67 x 112 x 50"
While at first glance these appear to be hands covered with moss, the forms are actually based on microscopic parts of some mosses, called lamellae. Their uncanny resemblance to human hands is a reminder that we humans are part of larger natural patterns. I continue to develop this idea at Roosevelt Community Center with spiral and dendritic patterns.

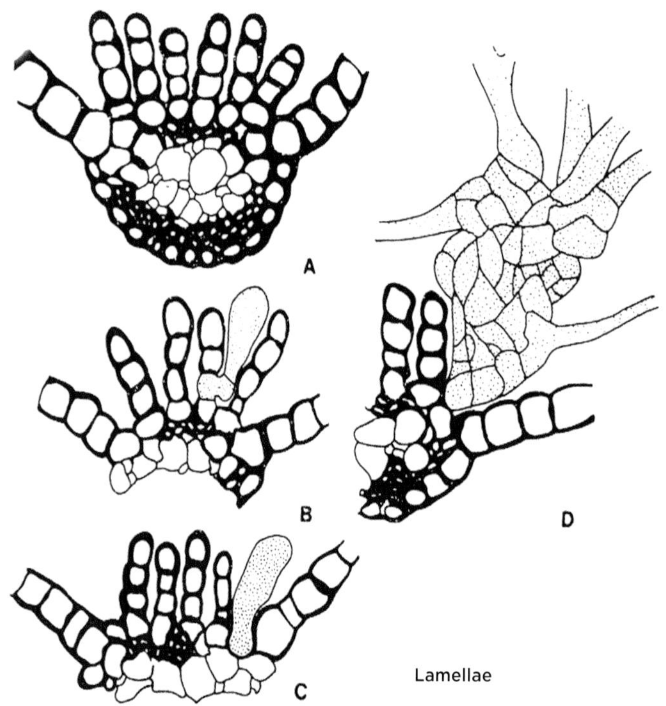

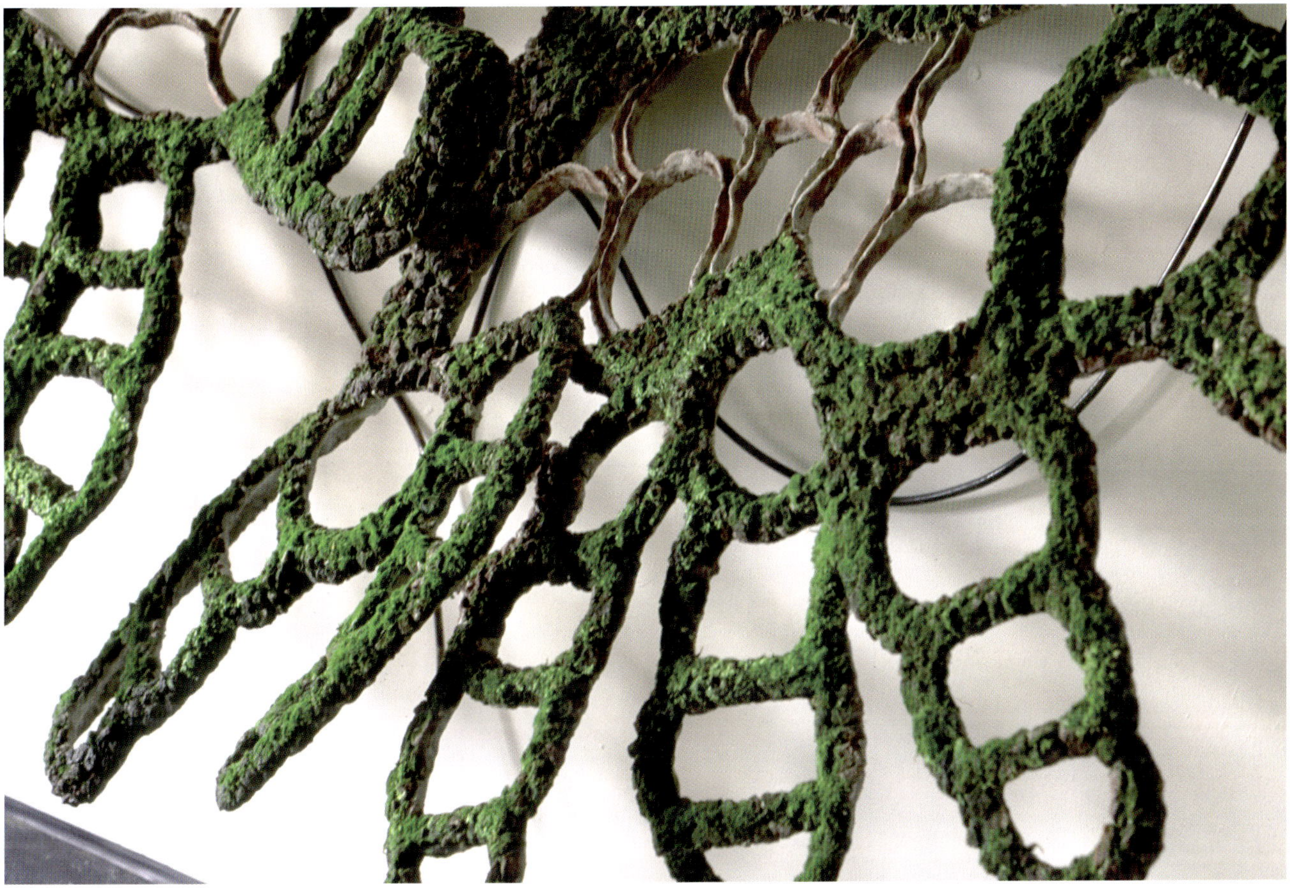

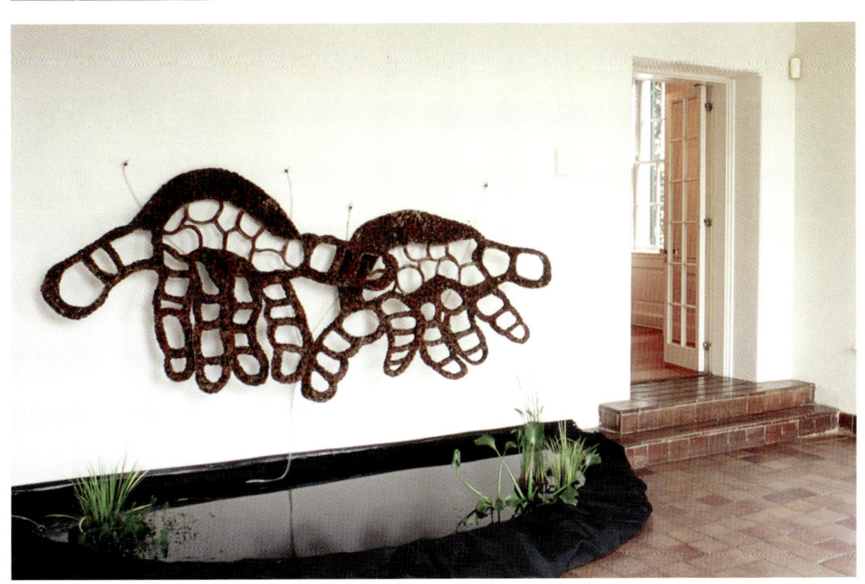

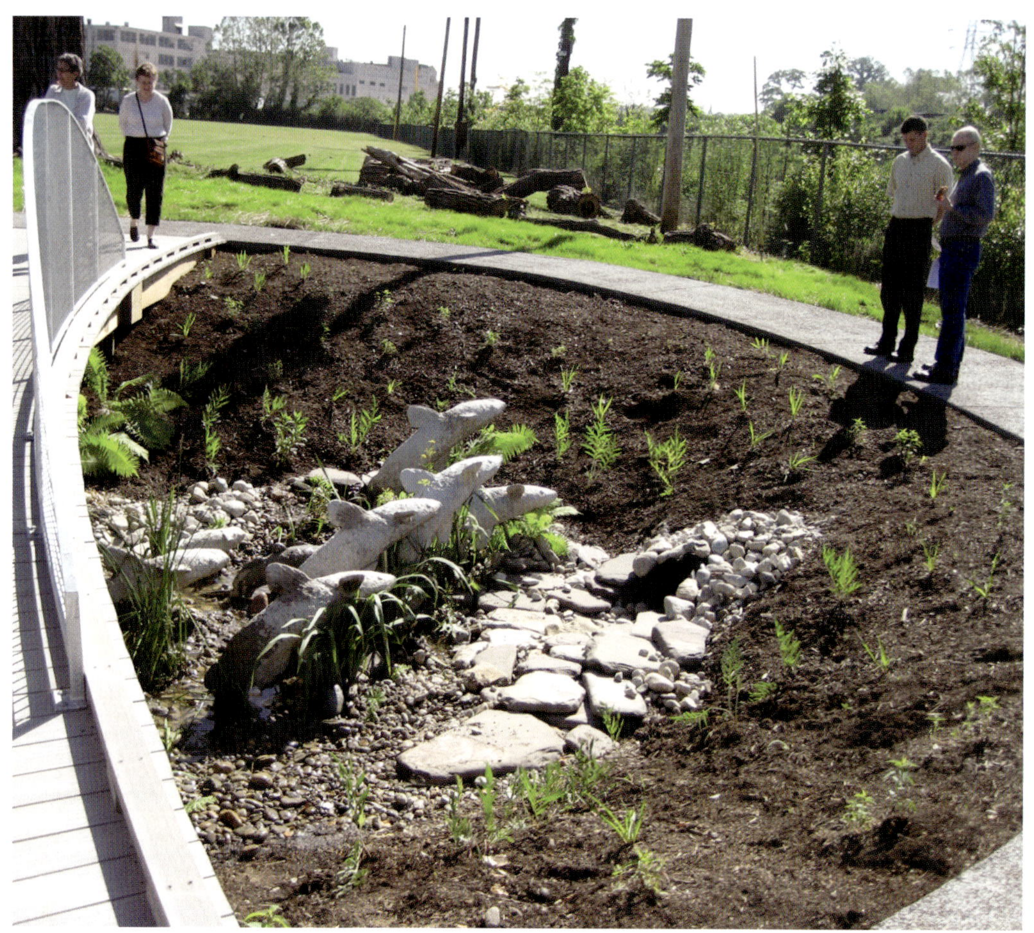

"I was laying down very elementary ideas about epistemology, that is about how we can know anything. In the pronoun we, I of course included the starfish and the redwood forest, the segmenting egg, and the Senate of the United States. And in the anything that these creatures variously know, I included "how to grow into five fold symmetry," "how to survive a forest fire," "how to learn," "how to write a constitution," "how to invent and drive a car," "how to count to seven," and so on."

GREGORY BATESON, Mind and Nature, A Necessary Unity

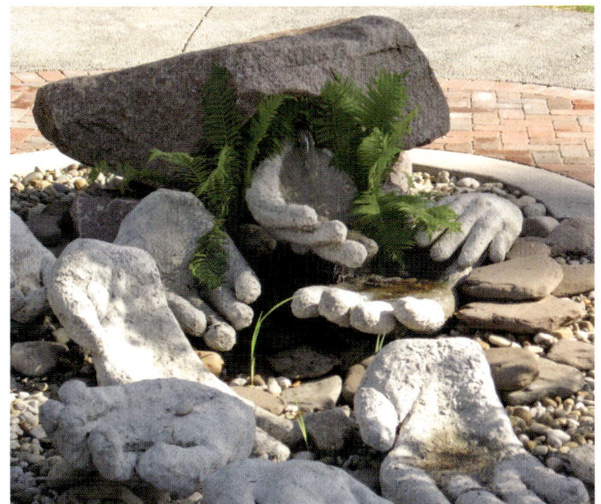

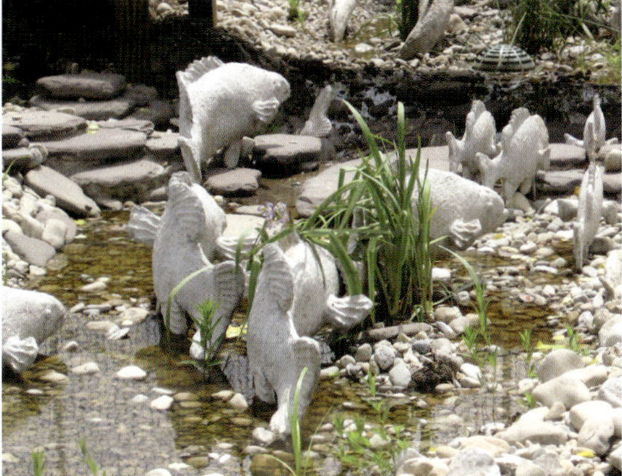

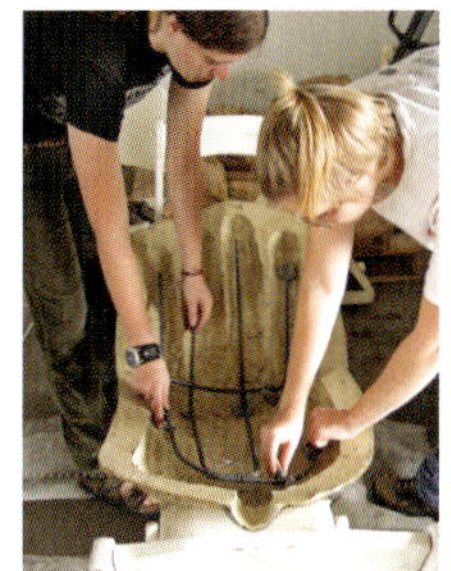

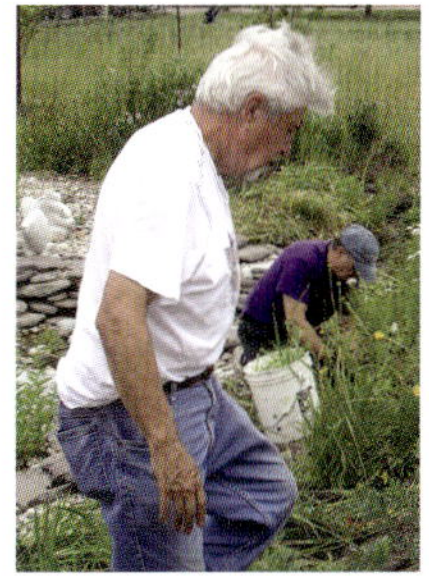

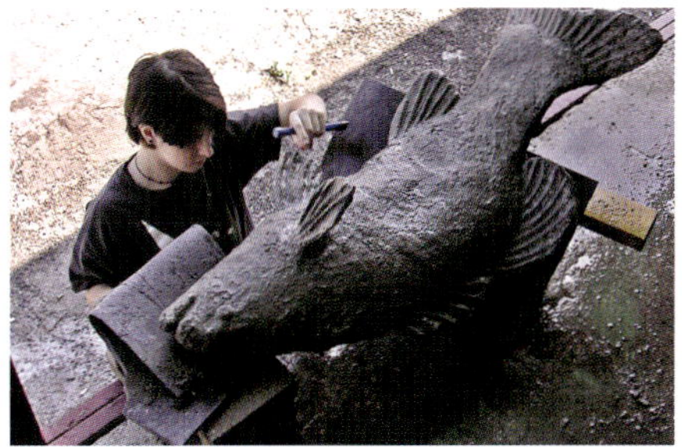

Laughing Brook demonstrates sustainable storm-water practices for sites along river banks. It also provokes questions. The Biosculptures™ start out as hands and in a kind of reverse evolution, gradually transform into six species of fish that would be there if the river were healthy. It asks, "What does the being of human mean?"

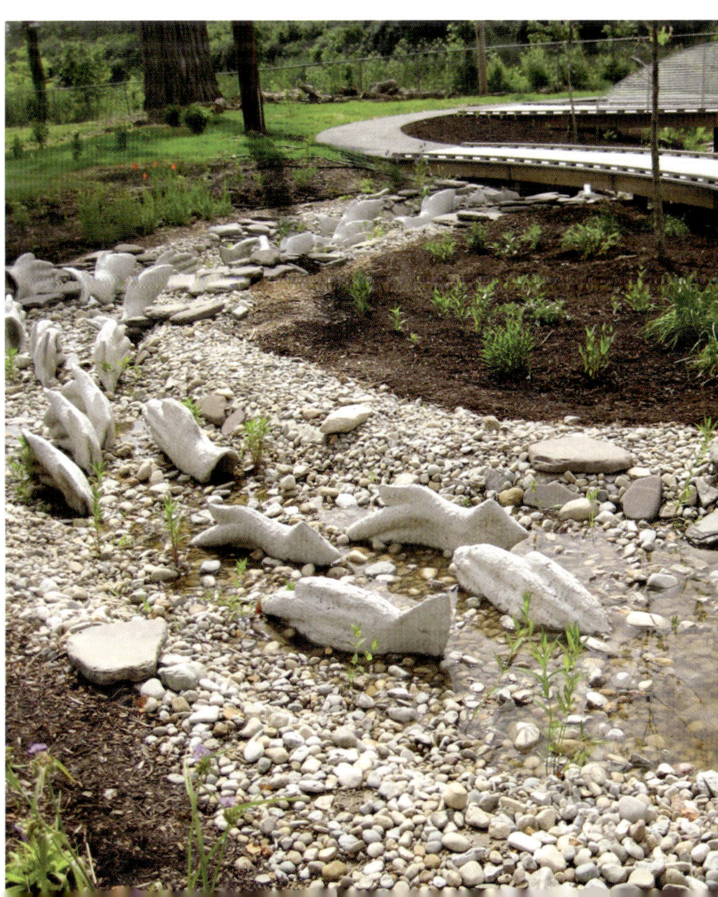

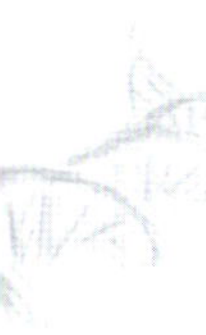

I've been trying to find ways to speak "water" for almost thirty years. JACKIE BROOKNER

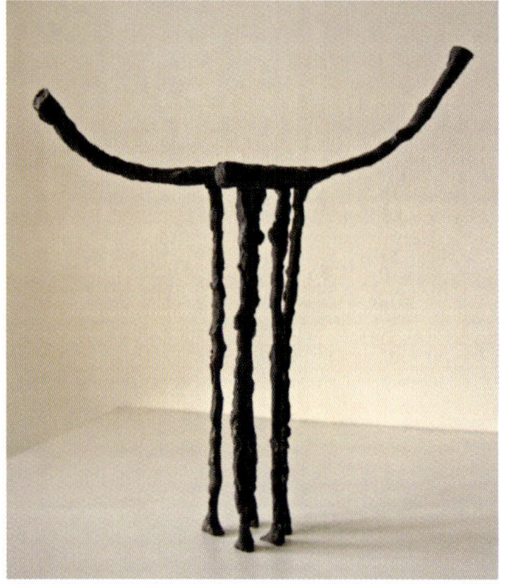

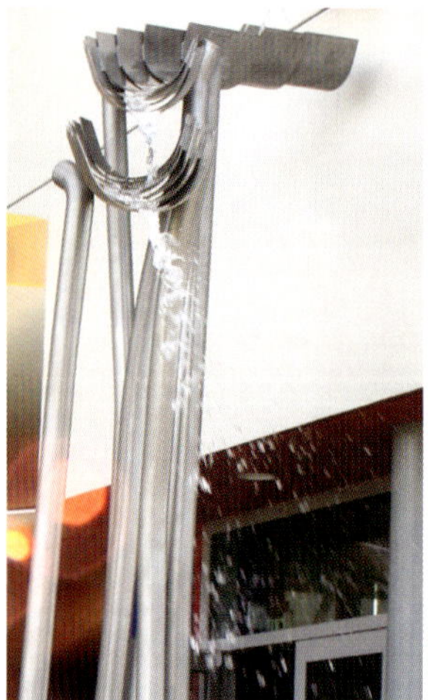

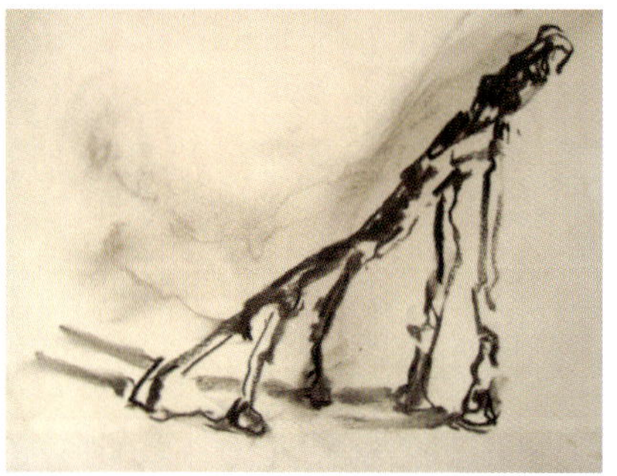

The first hints of the water chutes at Roosevelt Community Center were in my bronze sculptures and drawings of the early 1980s.

Elders' Cove Biosculpture™
2003-4
14 x 9 x 5.5'
The *Elders' Cove Biosculpture™* in Dreher Park, West Palm Beach Florida, is part of Elders' Cove landscape complex, a place for gathering and contemplation, on which I collaborated with Angelo Ciotti.

The issue here is also urban stormwater, but in this area that was once part of the Everglades the primary problem is flooding. This Biosculpture™ aerates and filters water in one of the new ponds built to detain stormwater. Its forms reflect the elaborate trunks of the Banyan trees abundant throughout the park. Elders' Cove landscape complex includes mounds built with the soil from the lake excavations, cypress islands that recall the original Everglades ecosystem, and a gathering area that honors the region's Seminole history.

I was recently surprised to find another harbinger of Urban Rain—an essay of mine published in 1999 where I was already thinking about branching patterns and spirals together. "… as I have been organizing my thoughts about how to get beyond dualisms I find myself making branching structures, and I keep getting confused, and the branches keep interweaving. And then, just now, as I have been thinking about it, I find my body also thinking, as I notice my arm and hand moving in a spiral motion above my notes. As the spiral grows its structure shows us where it has been, its particular moments in time and space. What's inside, what's outside are ambiguous, for what's outside now may be within later. And as it keeps turning, it returns, but never to the same place. A whole, but open ended, dynamic—perhaps it can help us find a way to more differentiated unities and less threatening differences."

JACKIE BROOKNER, *Natural Reality*, catalog essay

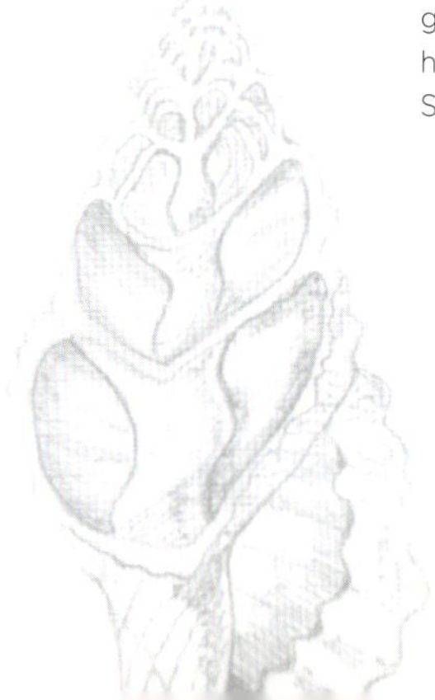

34

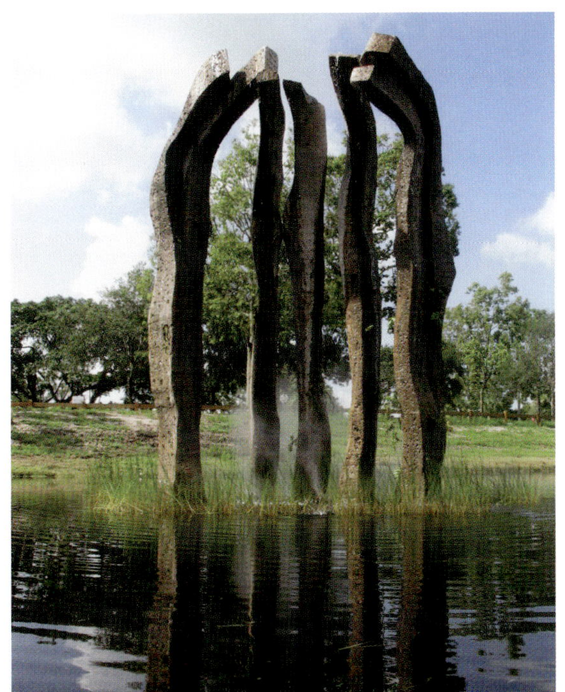

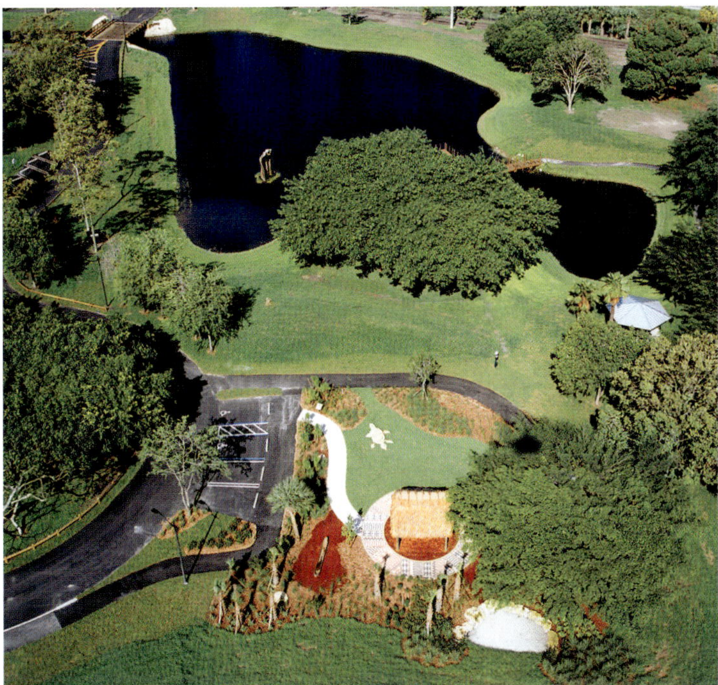

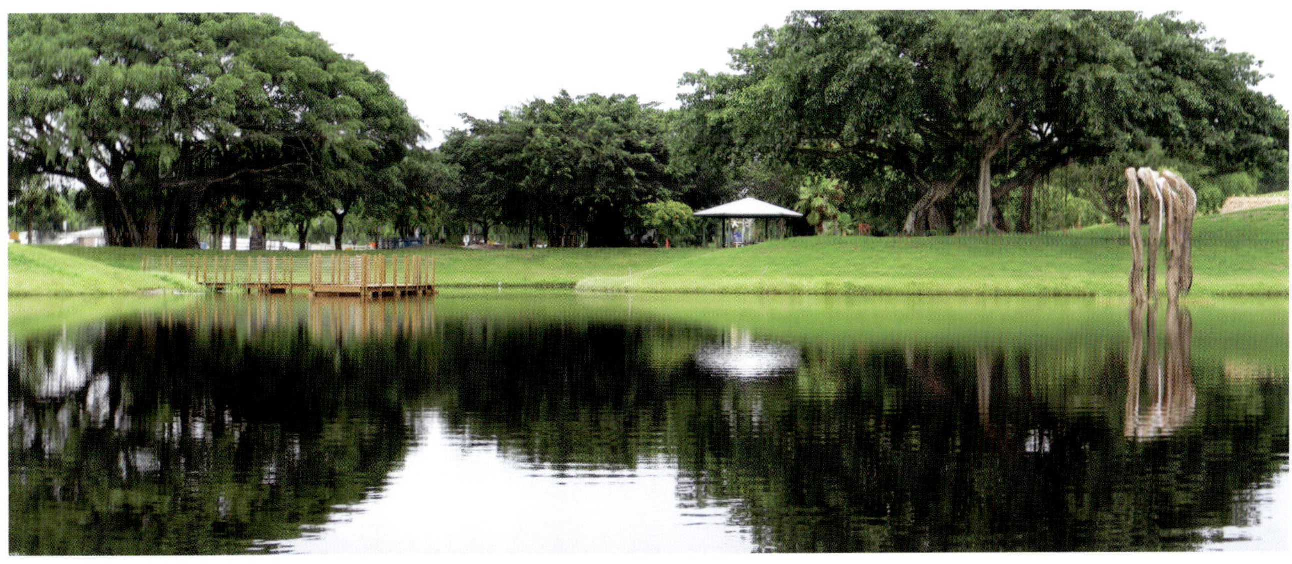

the true nature of poetry. The drive to connect.
The dream of a common language. ADRIENNE RICH

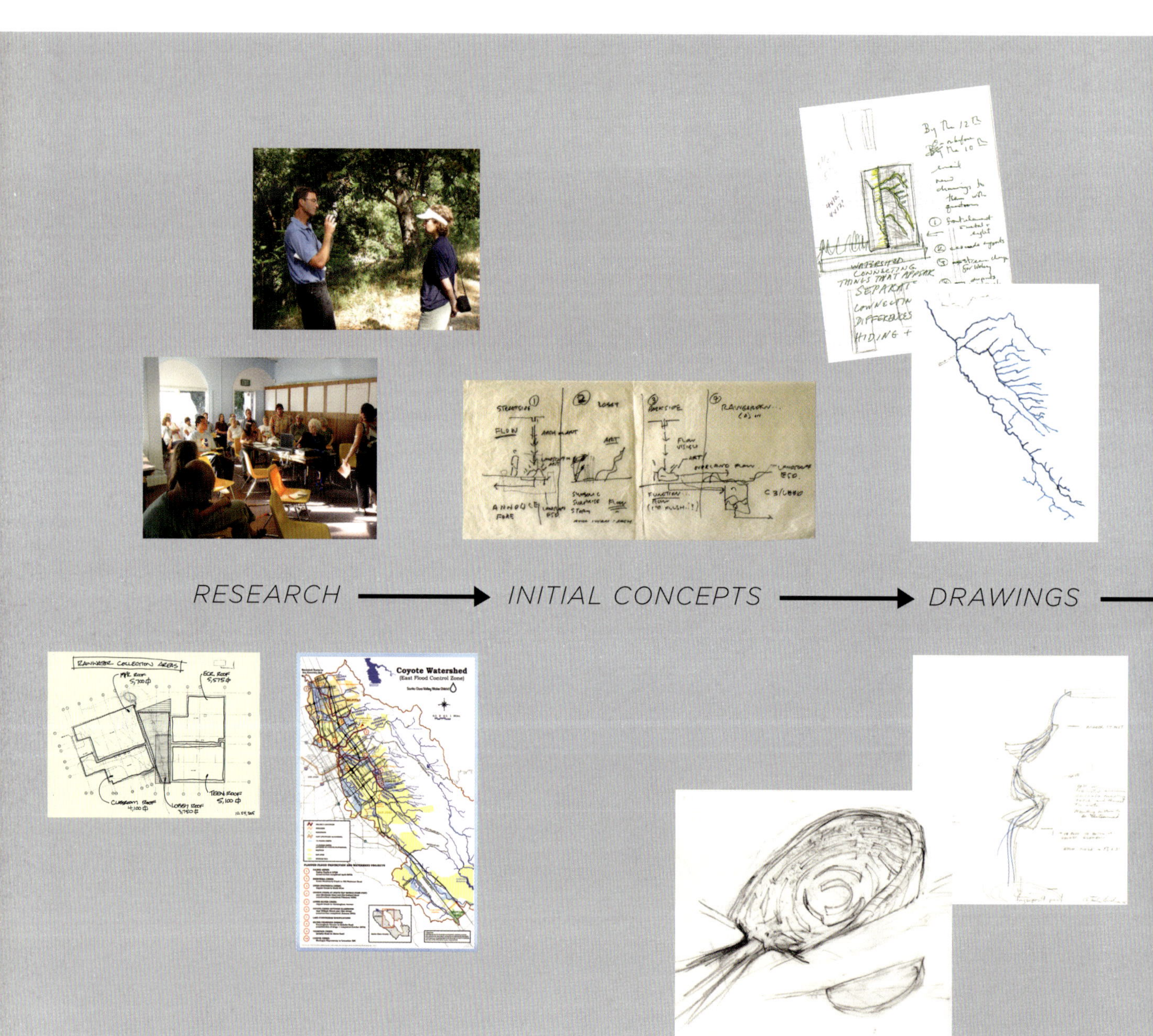

RESEARCH
INITIAL CONCEPTS
DRAWINGS

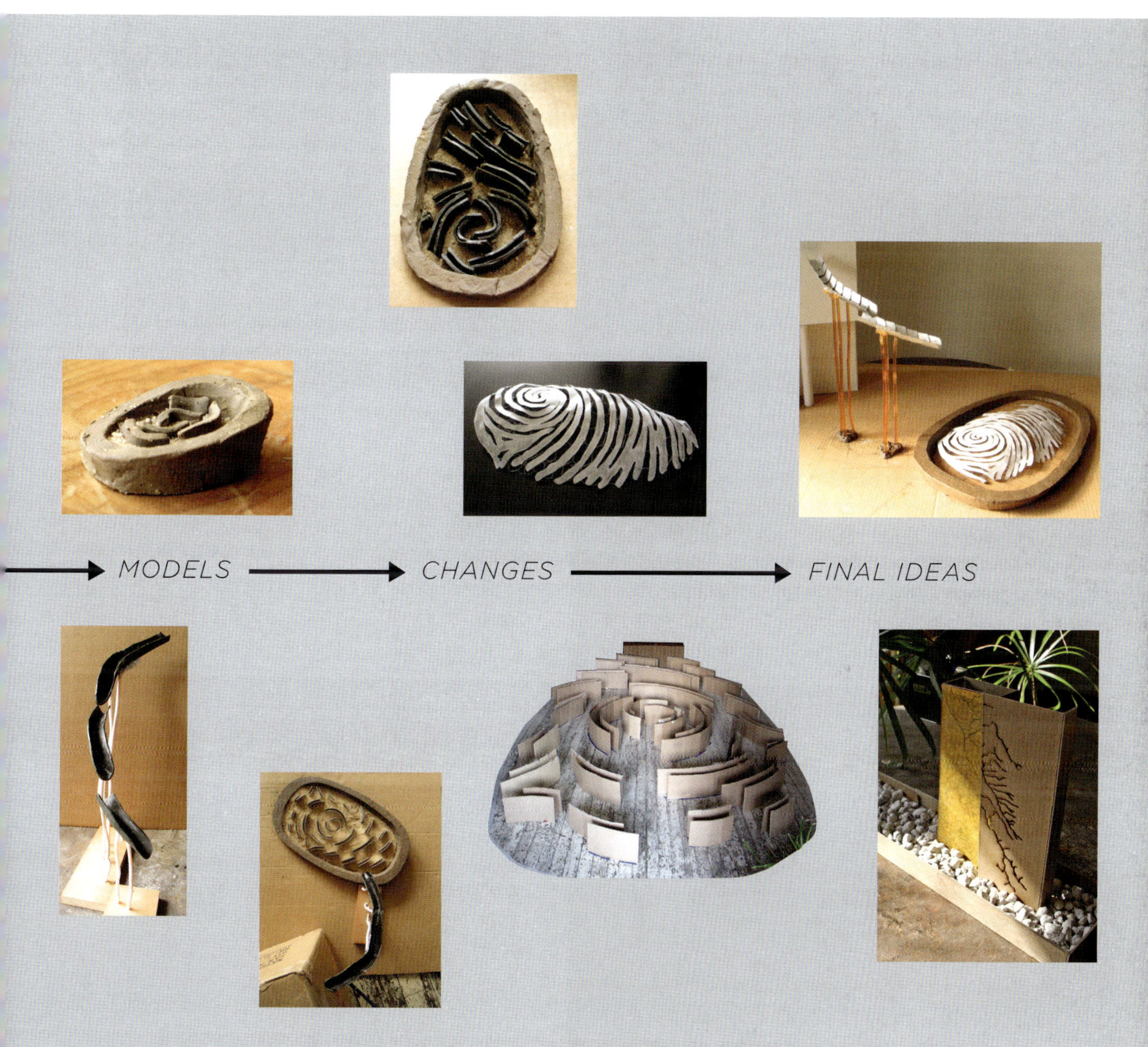

PROJECT DEVELOPMENT

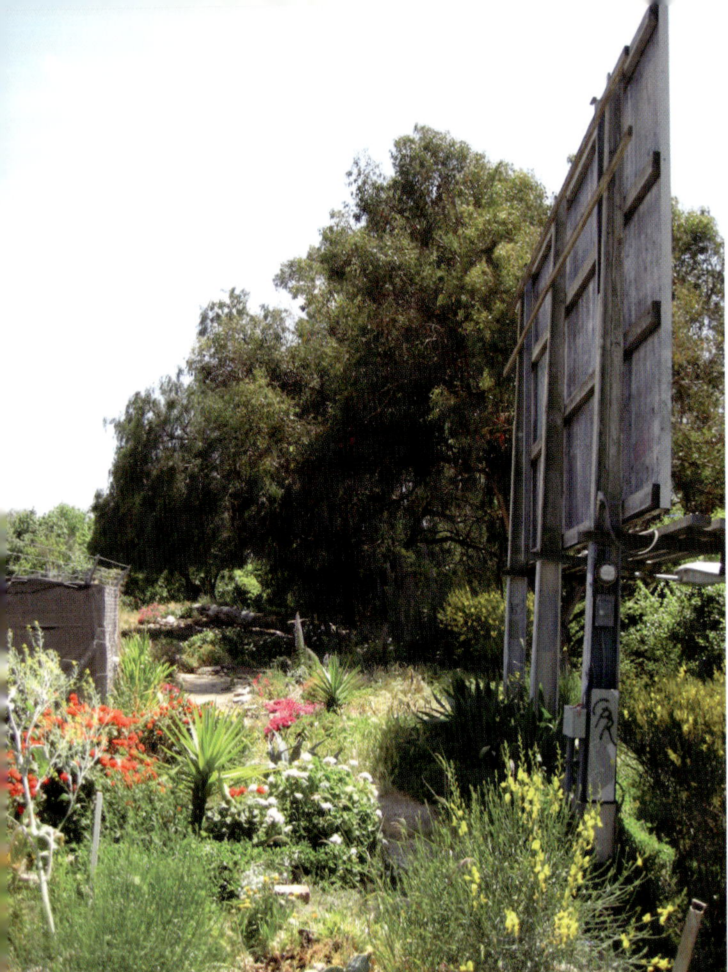

I begin by listening, and asking lots of questions. From my first conversations with people in the community it was immediately clear that they saw the Community Center as part of Roosevelt Park, and Coyote Creek as the heart of the park. People said they love Coyote Creek and that it was one of the few places in the city where they could experience nature. Just how much people love the creek is obvious right at the 20th Street Bridge on Santa Clara. Well used walking paths wind through this beautiful planted and tended garden in the shadow of a billboard on the banks of the creek.

At my briefings with the architects, the City Environmental Services staff, park and City representatives, I heard about Coyote Creek again—about the need to protect the creek from stormwater runoff flowing from the roof of the building and the paved surfaces of its parking lots, sidewalks and driveways.

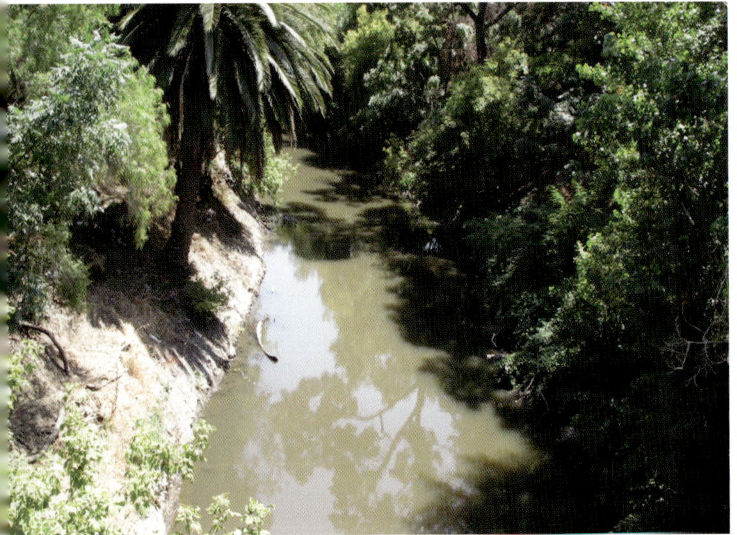

Left

A neighborhood garden at the top of the bank

Coyote Creek near the 20th Street Bridge

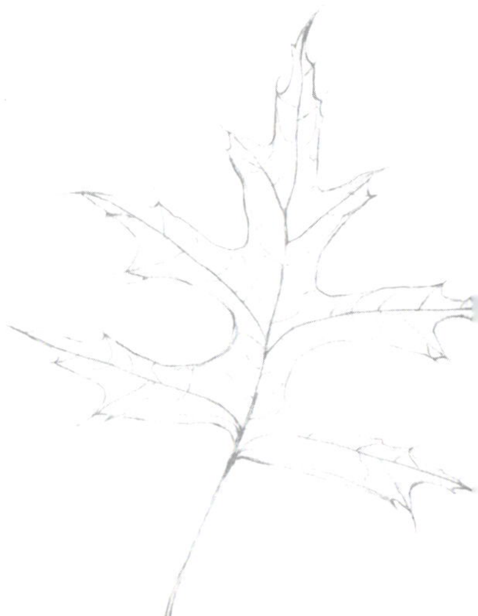

It was clear I needed to explore Coyote Creek and learn about the watersheds of the South Bay area. Who better could guide me along Coyote Creek than the San Jose Environmental Services Department Biologist James Downing and Watershed Protection specialist Anastasia Aziz? James made several references to "touching water" which stayed with me and inspired the project.

I met with Larry Wilson, Director of District 4 at Santa Clara Valley Water District, who generously told me about the history of the water supply for San Jose, about local geology, and about how there is no intergenerational memory of droughts and floods. He said Coyote Creek is the most important water course in the Valley, because it has the largest watershed. He also talked about how the water level of Coyote Creek dropped between 6 and 13 feet from 1900 to 1960 because so much water was being drawn from underground for agriculture. When I asked him what he most wanted people to know about water, he said, "Streams and rivers are living things and need to be treated with respect."

Larry Johmann and Roger Castillo, citizen stewards of San Jose's waterways, were full of stories about the creeks they love and know so intimately. "Every section of the river has its own smell." "There used to be a beach at 17th and Santa Clara." "In the 30's, you could walk across the salmon in the River, there were so many." "Salmon don't know what gabions are. They don't know what wire is. They go after the rocks to make a nest." "Without water you have nothing."

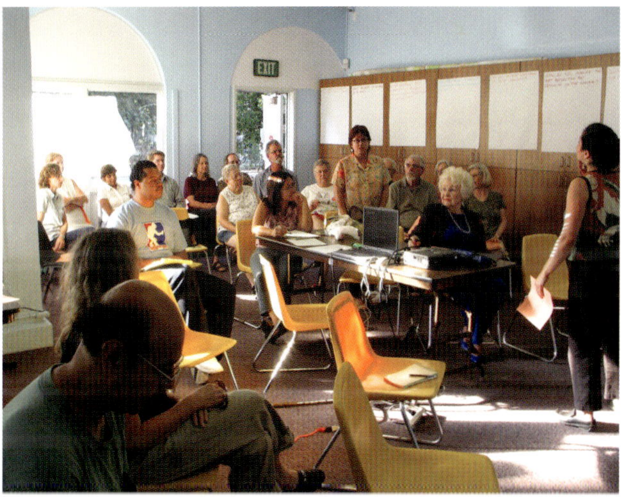

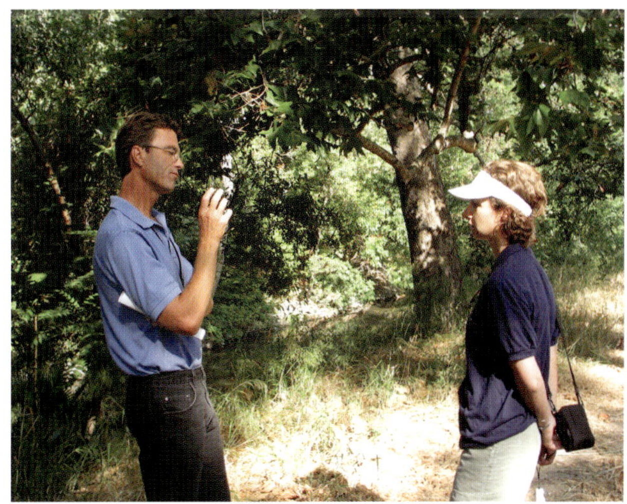

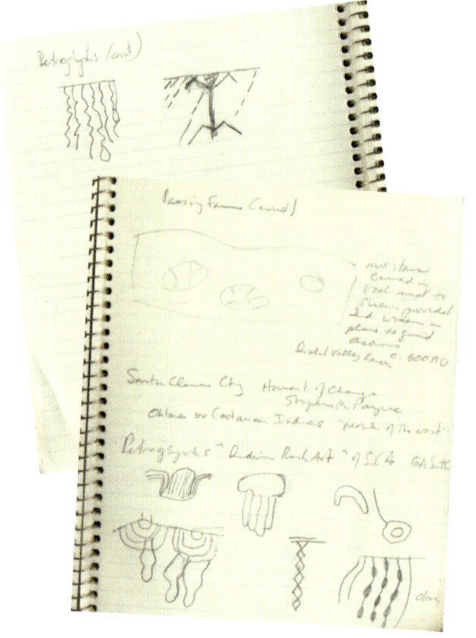

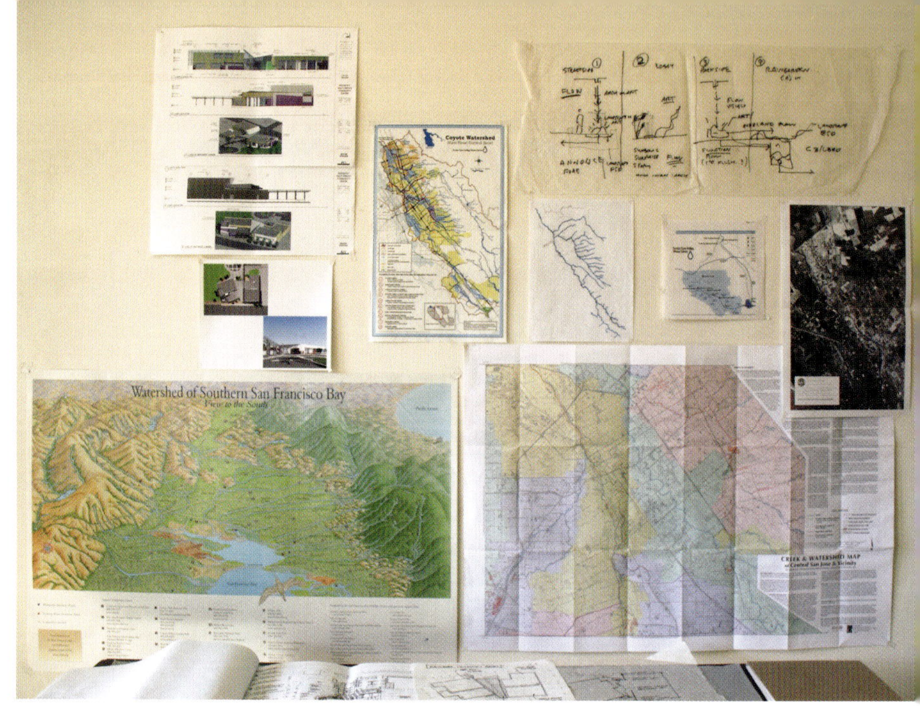

Sketch Book
Local Native
American petroglyphs
about water

Studio Wall
Thinking about the
building and site
within the Coyote
Creek Watershed

Right

Group 4's drawings of
the roof's rainwater
collection areas

Far right

Santa Clara Valley
Water District map
of Coyote Creek
watershed

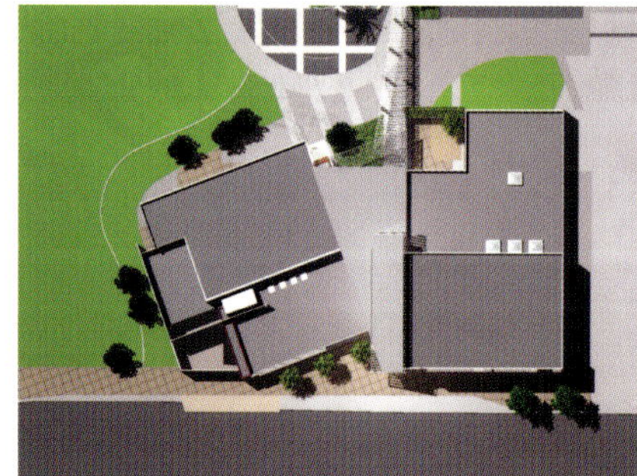

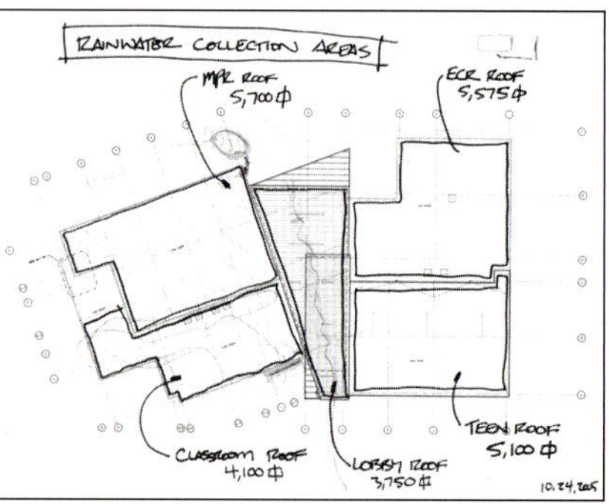

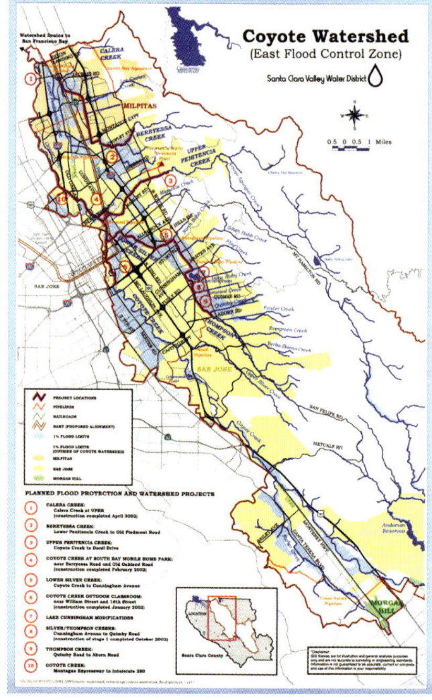

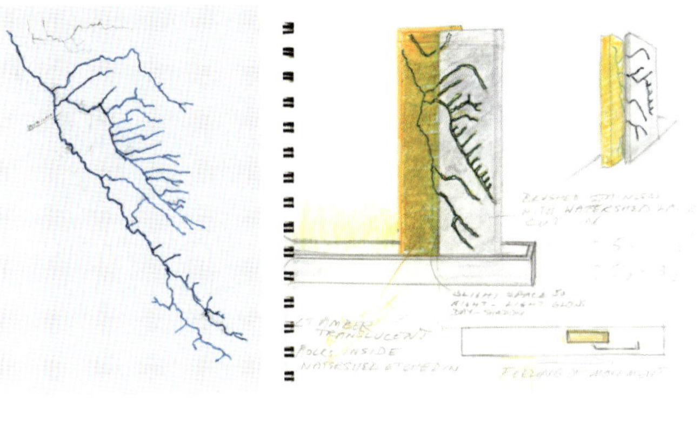

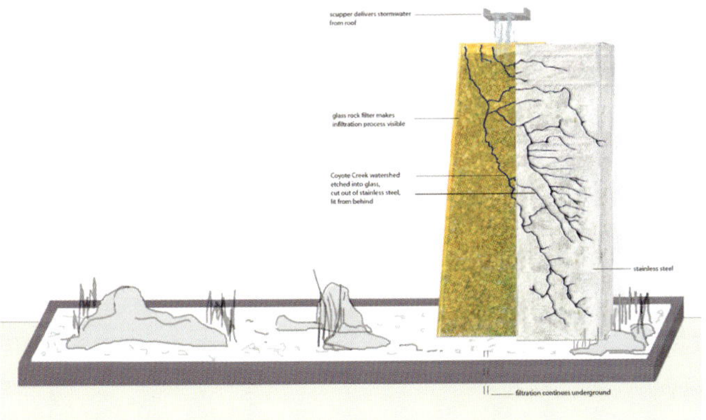

Working out ideas for the *Coyote Creek Filter*: from hand sketches to computer drawings, to a 9" high cardboard model in the studio (1"=1').

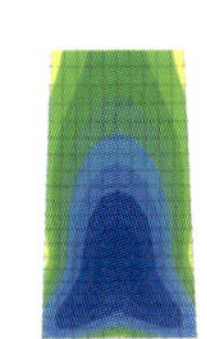

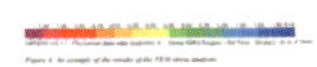

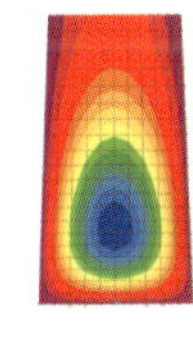

Engineering analysis of the stresses on the filter glass from the rocks and water behind it

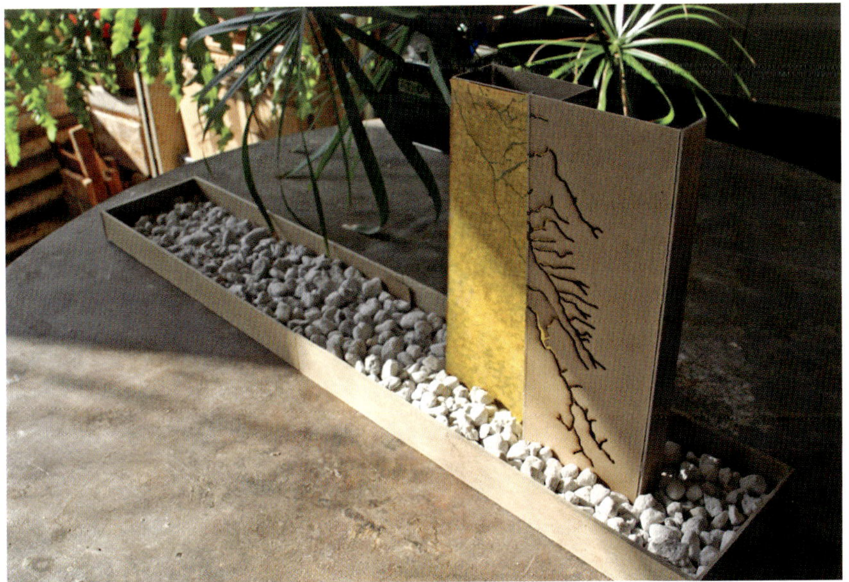

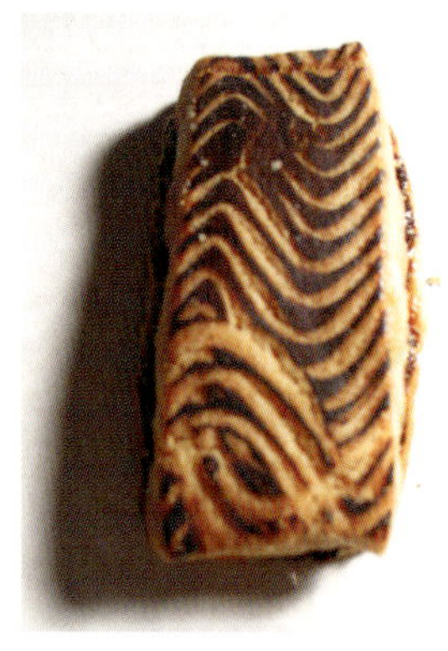
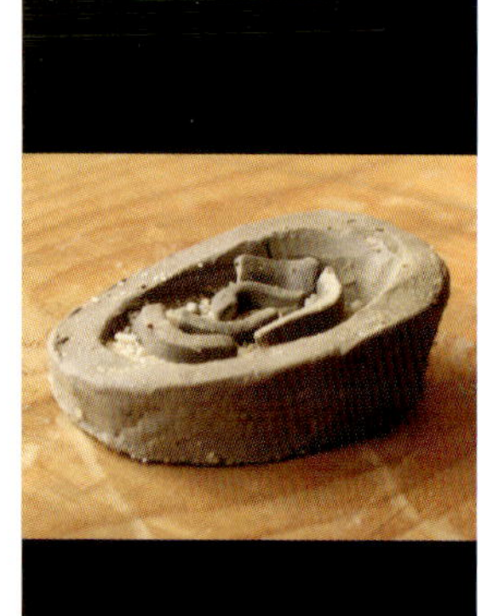
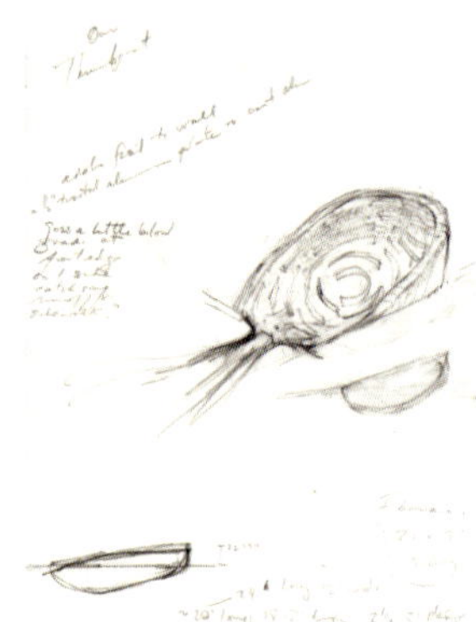

The wave pattern on a breakfast pastry was the first clue that led to the spiral patterns of our fingertips as an image. Studies started with sketches and tiny models, then to larger models and finally to a full size cardboard model on the studio floor.

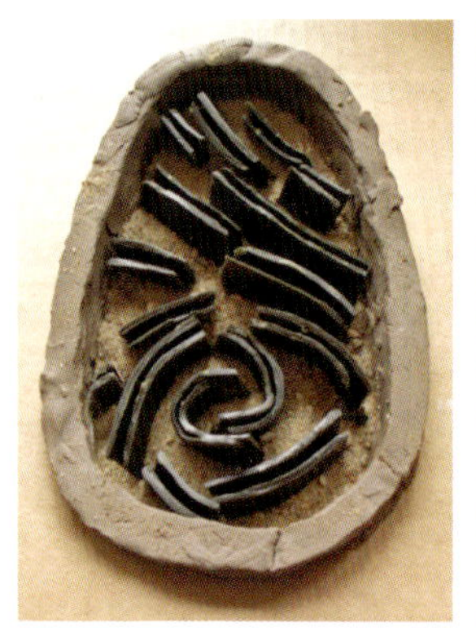
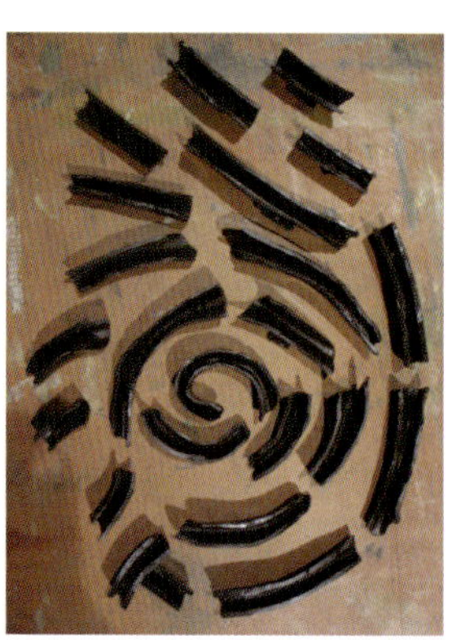
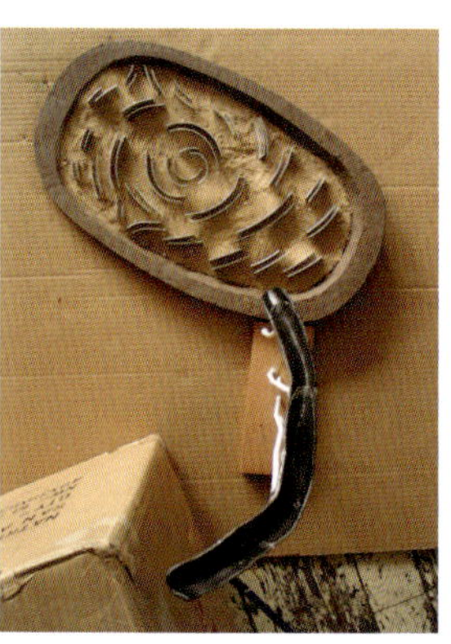

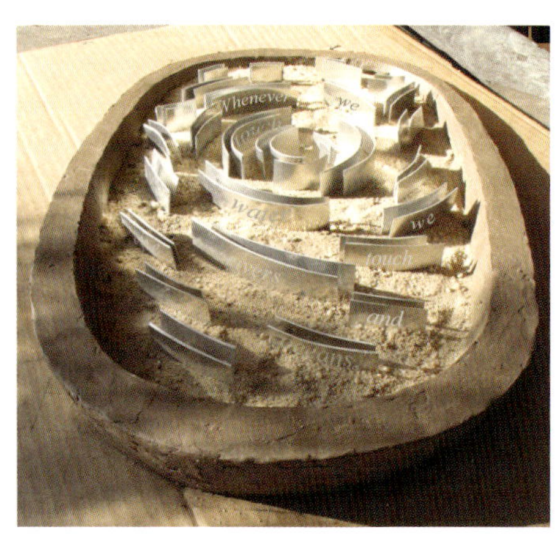
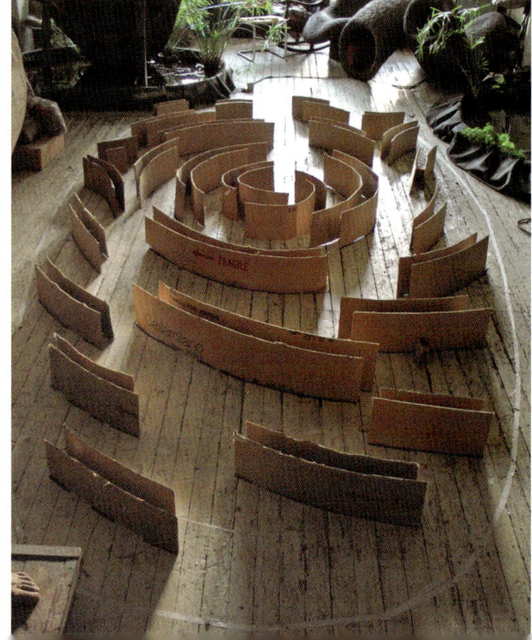

After completing
the full scale model,
safety concerns came
up that sent me
back to the drawing
board, and led to a
whole new concept
for the thumbprint. I
abstracted this from
my actual thumbprint
in the drawing
(bottom right) and
explored it with the 15"
paper model *(below)*.

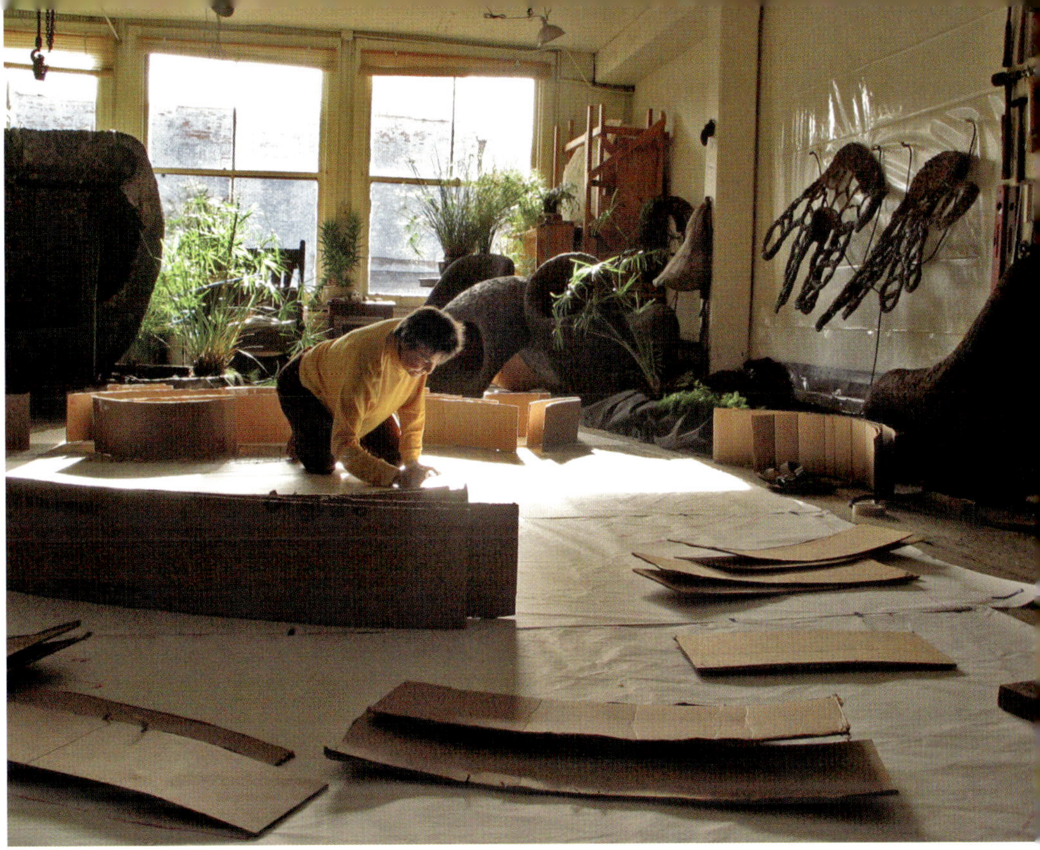

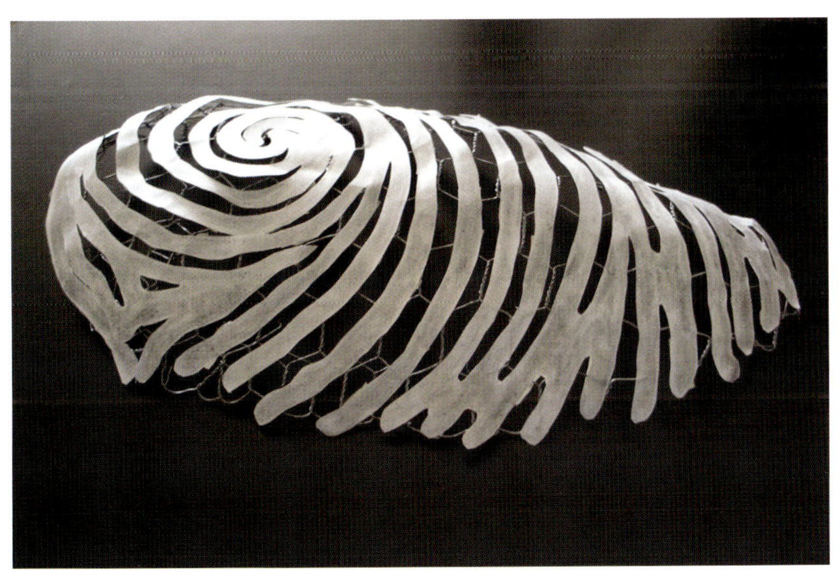

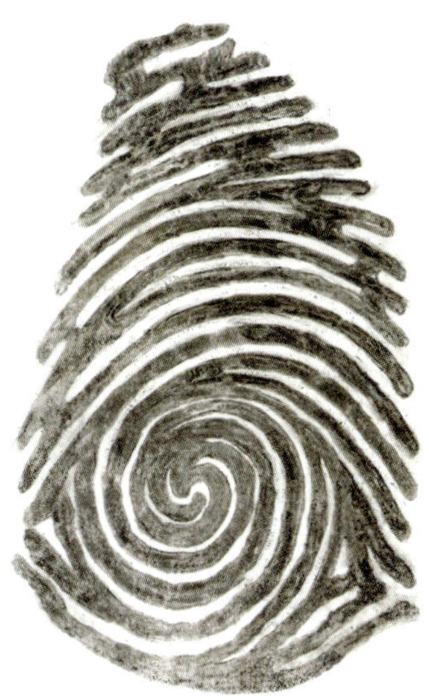

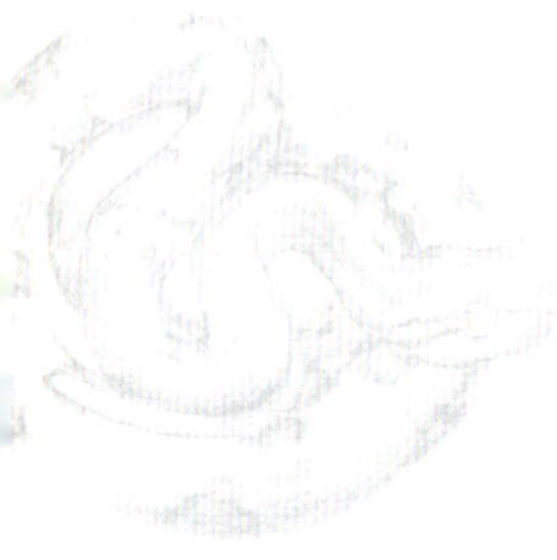

Model

The 1:1 scale model for the Thumbprint filter with the sloped seating wall and the water chutes

Drawing

Computer studies for different views of the thumbprint and the under ground structure

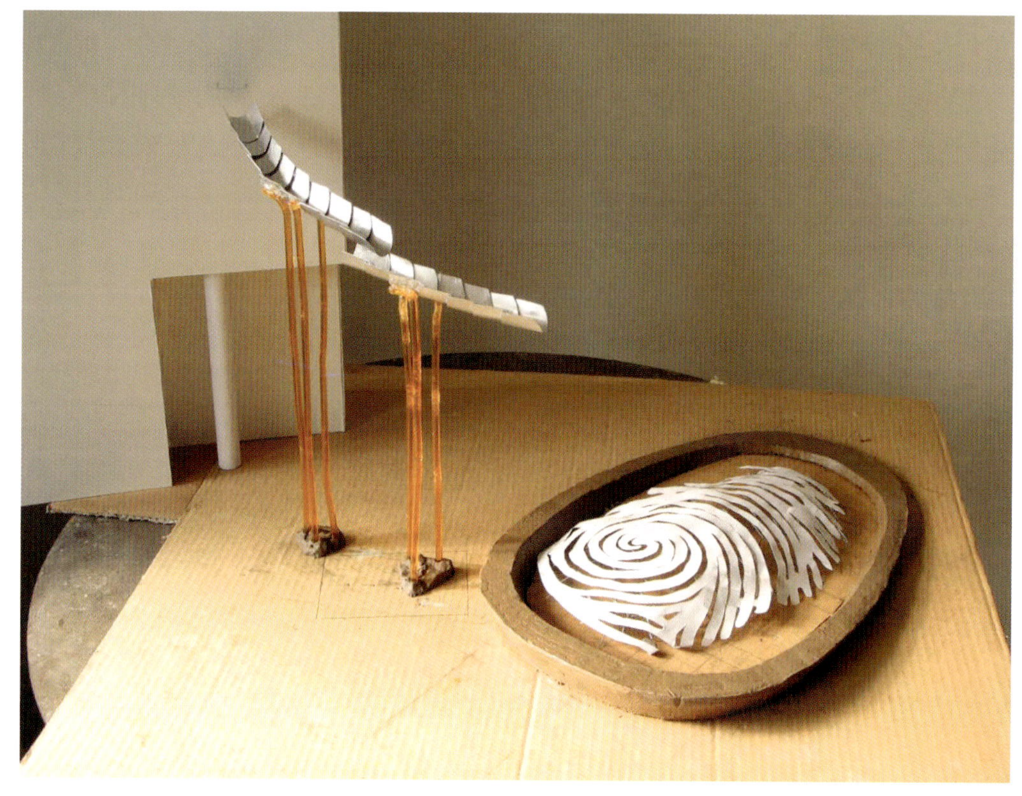

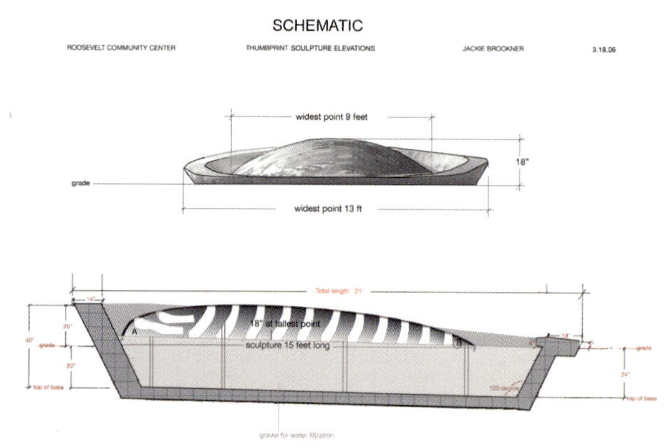

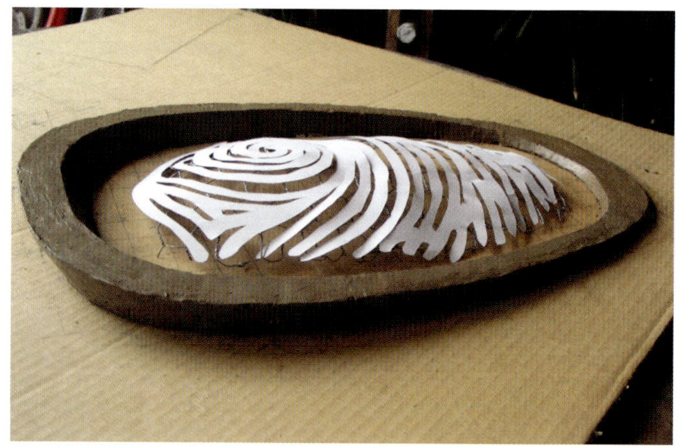

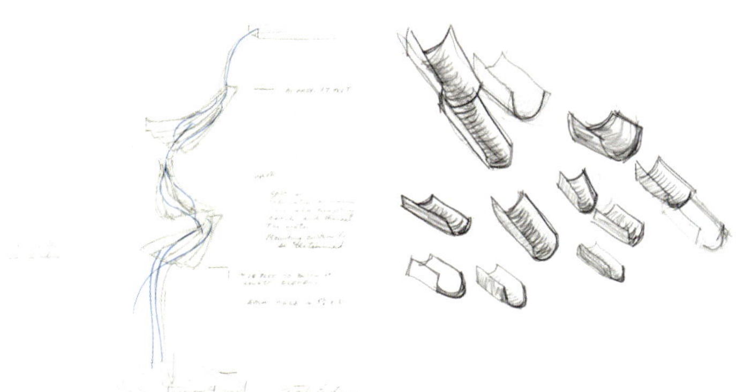

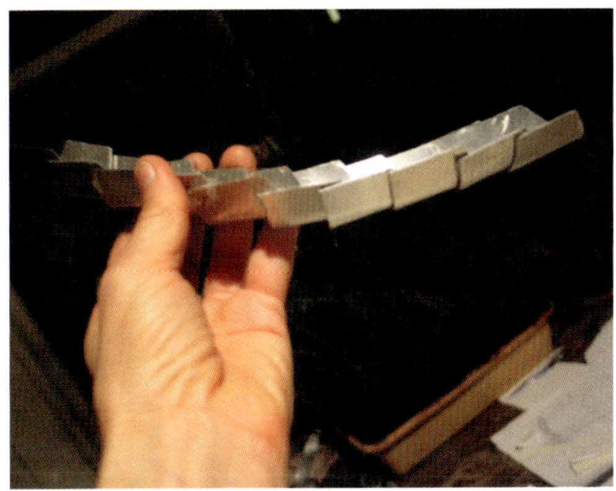

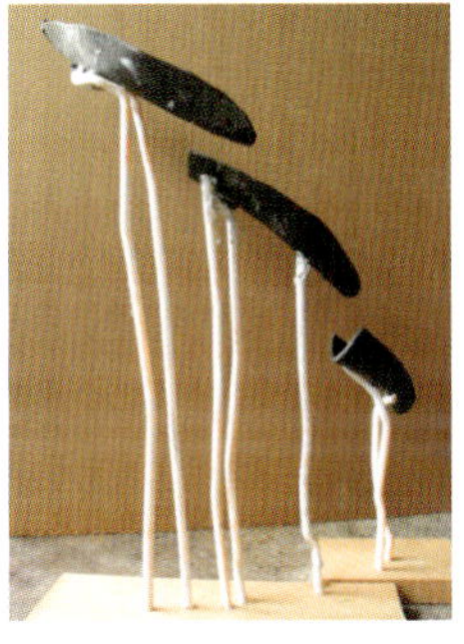

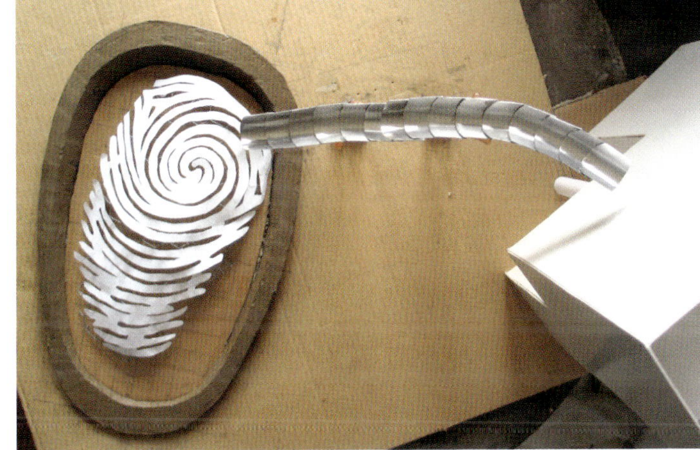

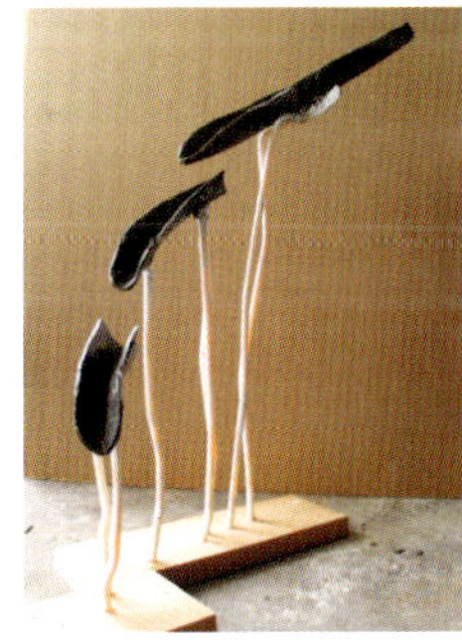

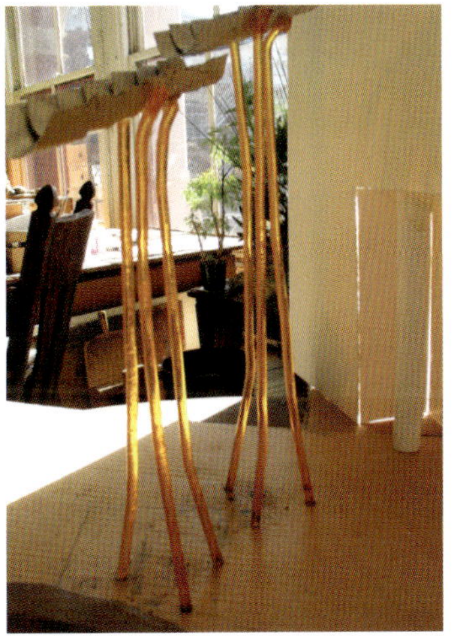

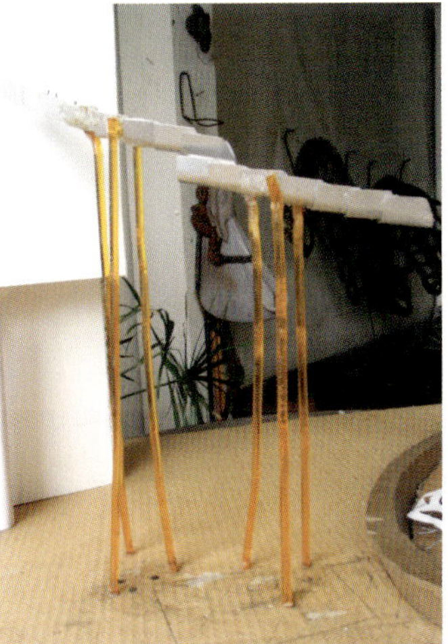

Ideas for the water chutes developed over several versions of drawings and 1:1 models, needing to change as the thumbprint changed.

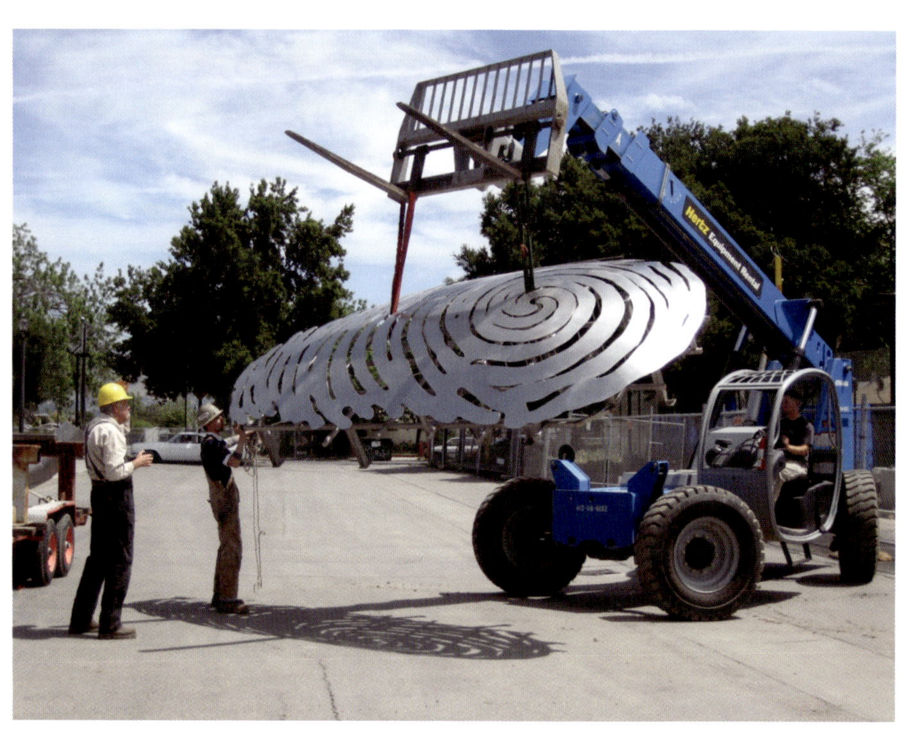

Water is our first mirror. H. LEFEBRE

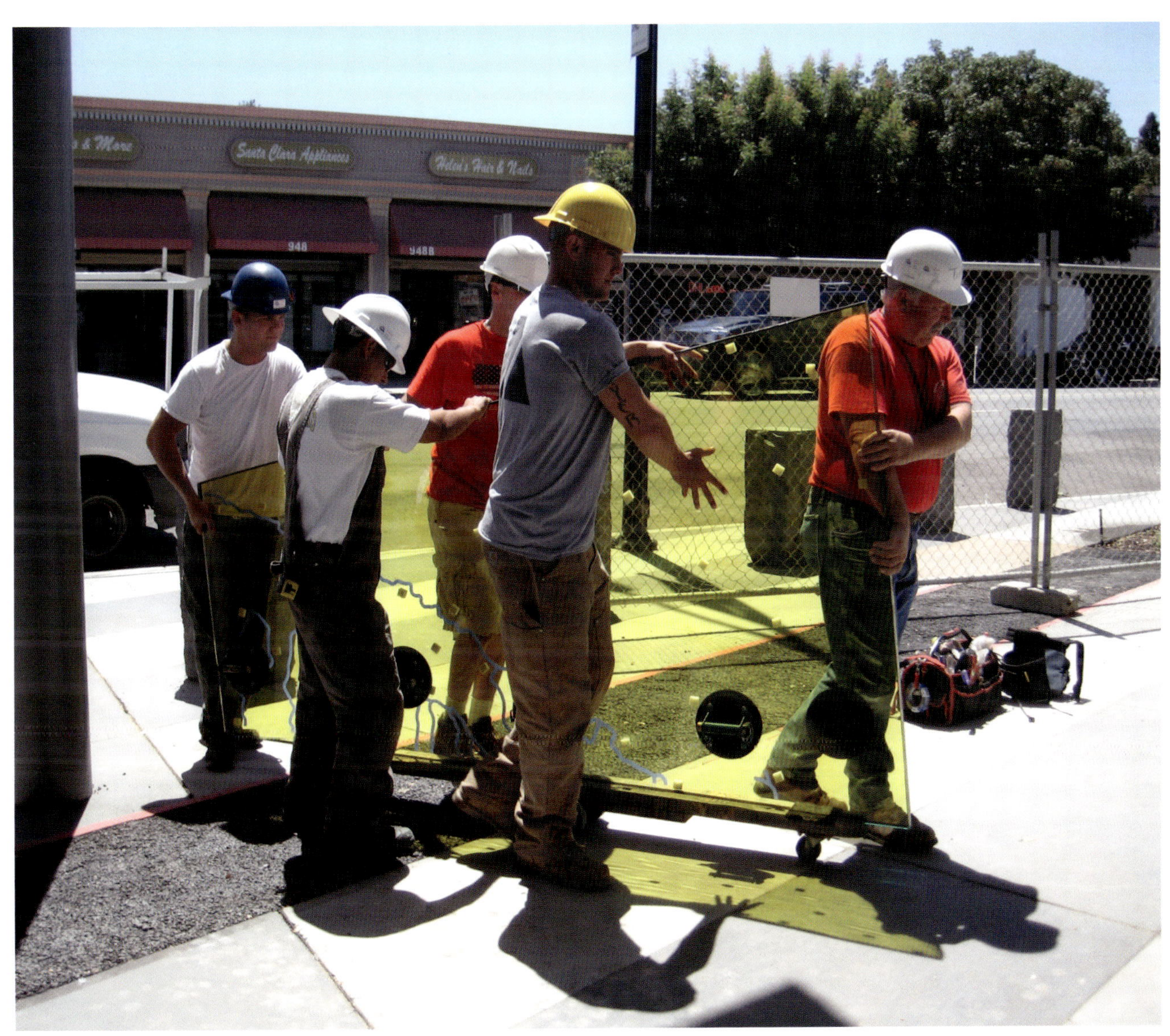

FABRICATION AND INSTALLATION

Installing the heavy 1 and 3/8 inch thick glass panel required great care and great coordination, while filling the pumice stone asked for great patience.

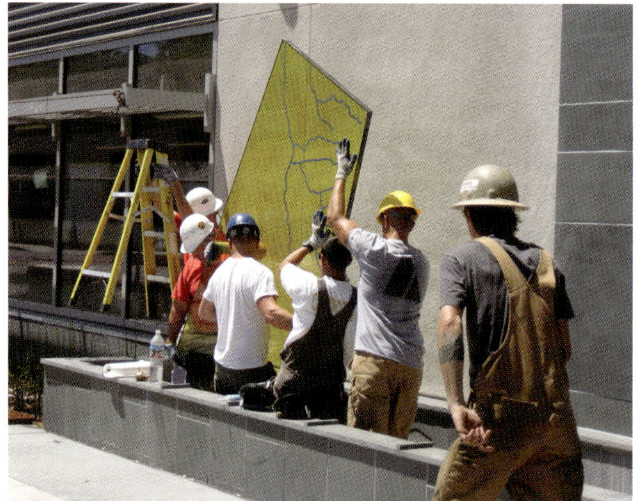

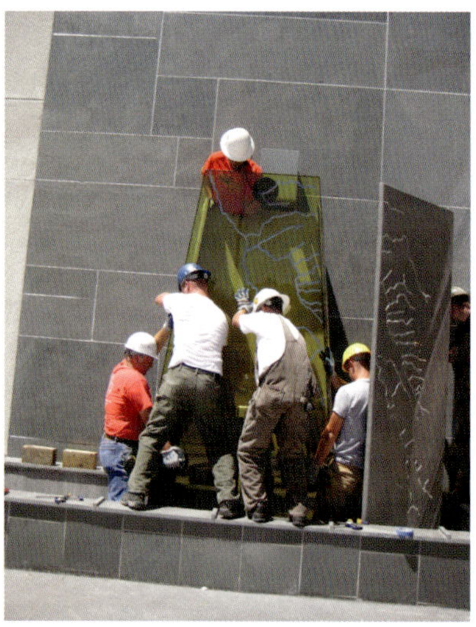

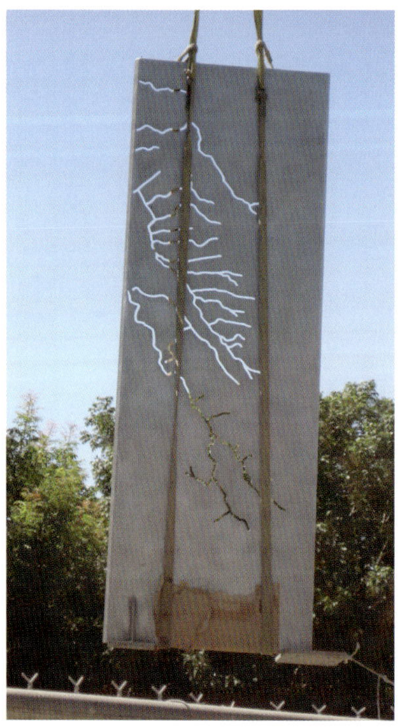

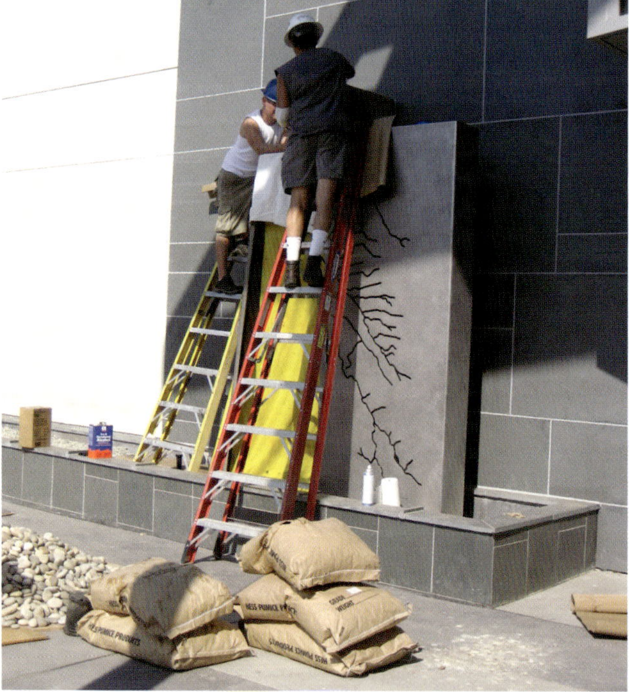

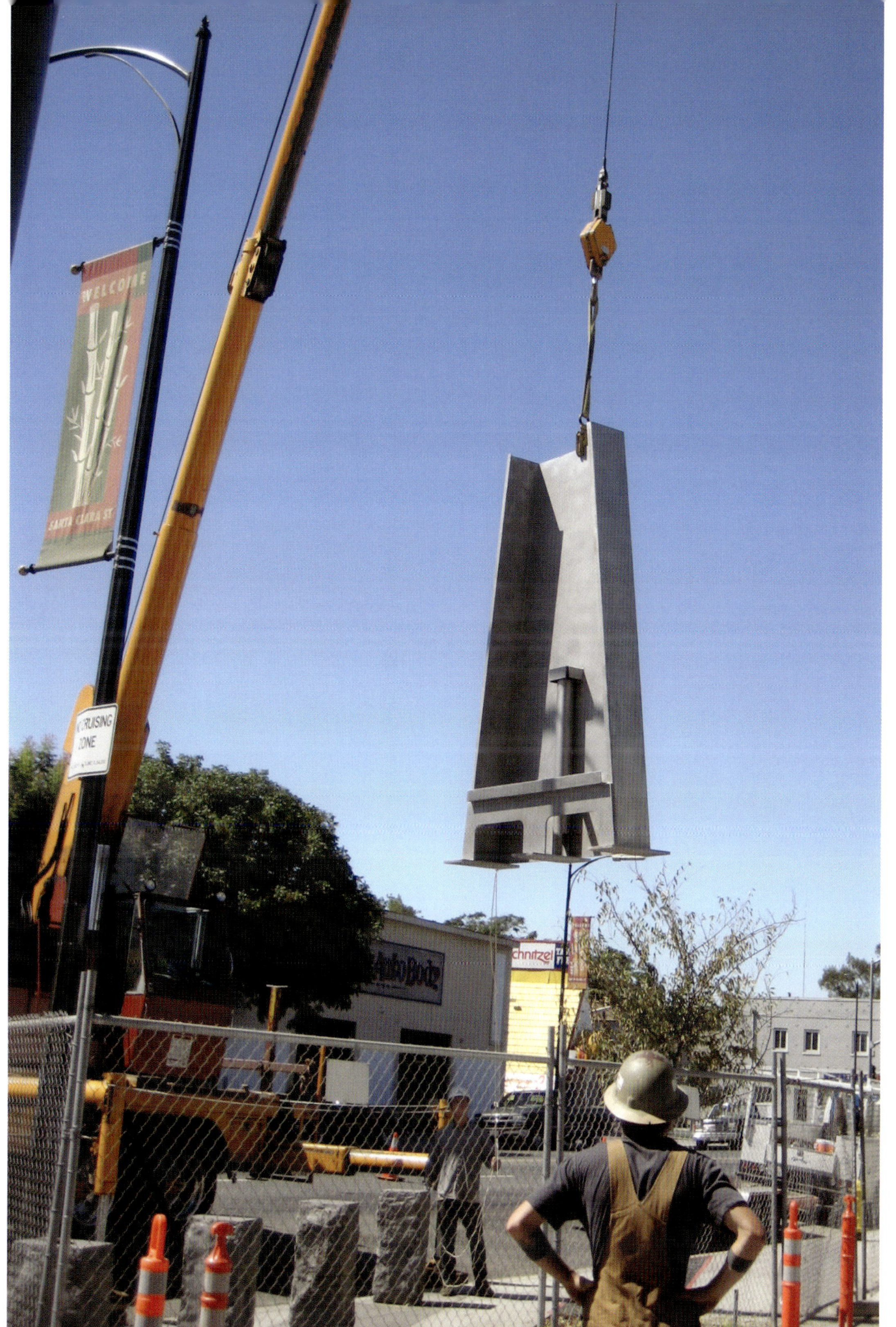

Craning the stainless steel housing for the glass into place.

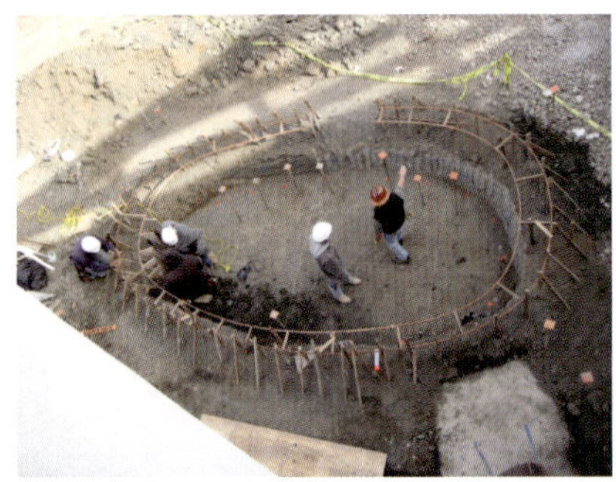
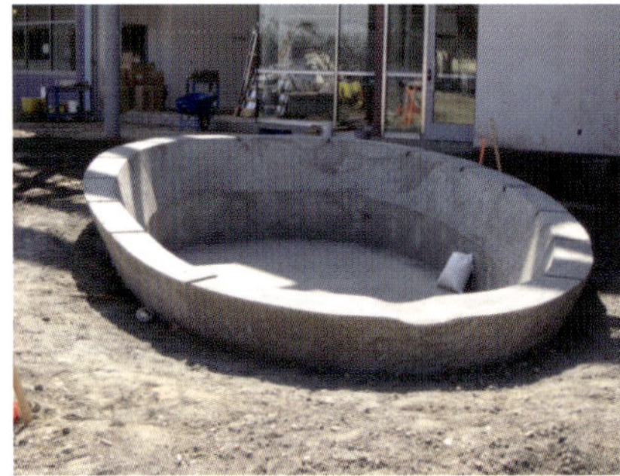
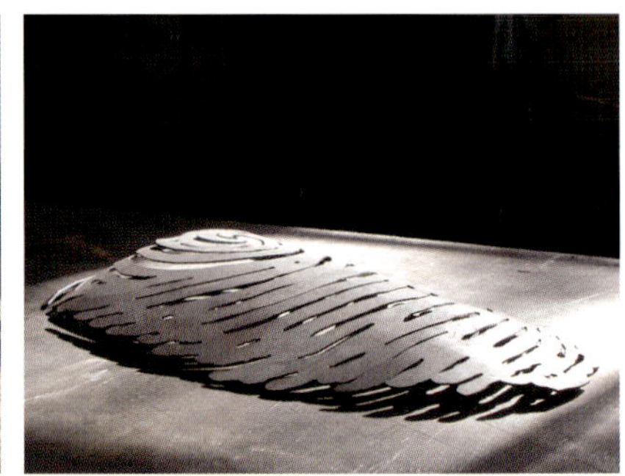
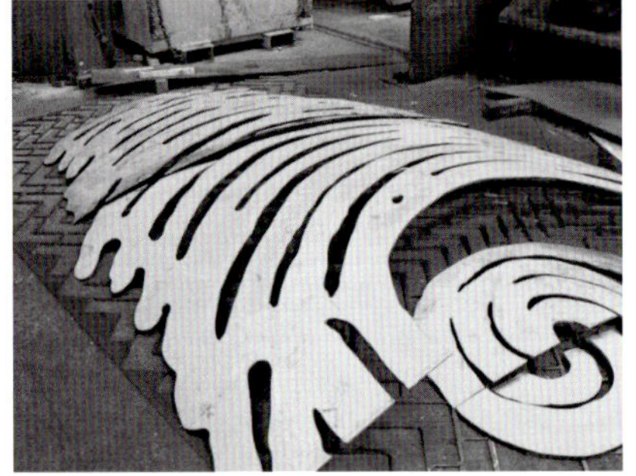
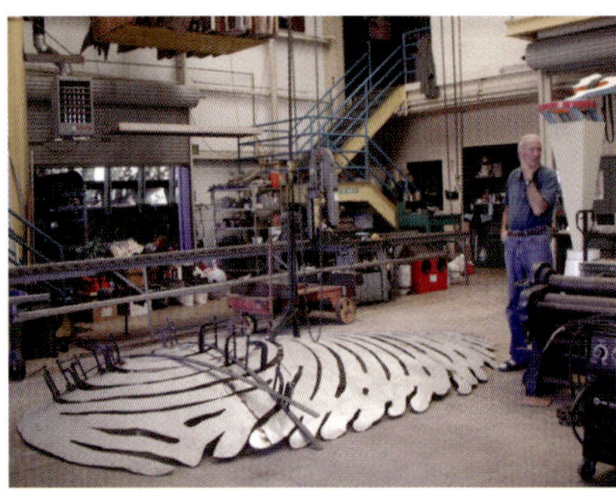
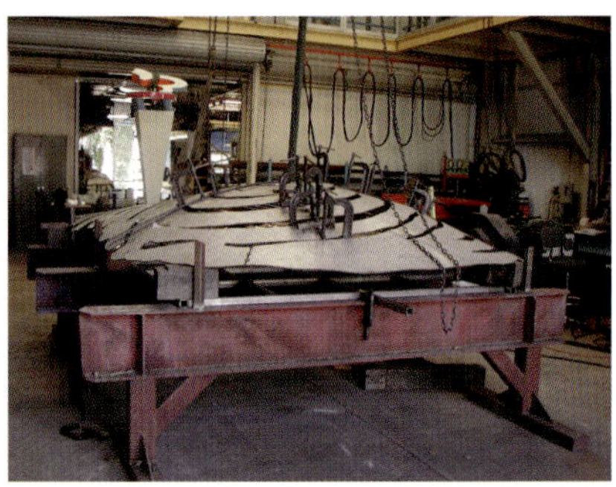
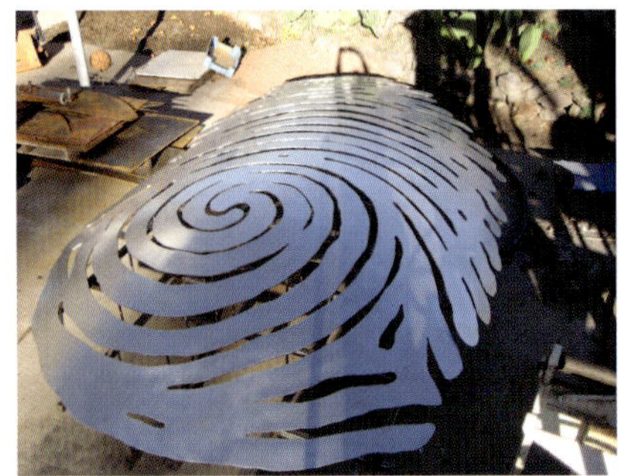
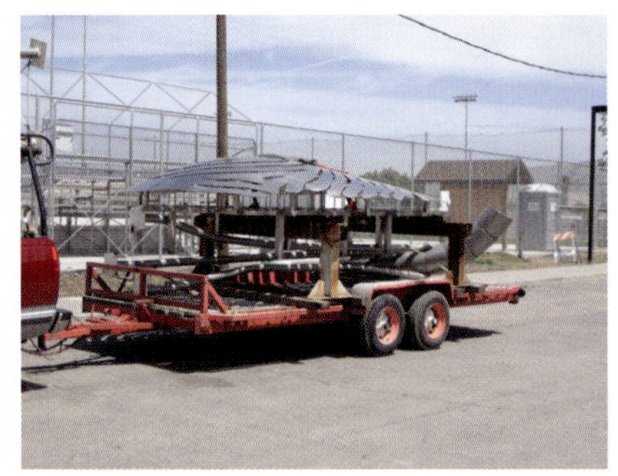
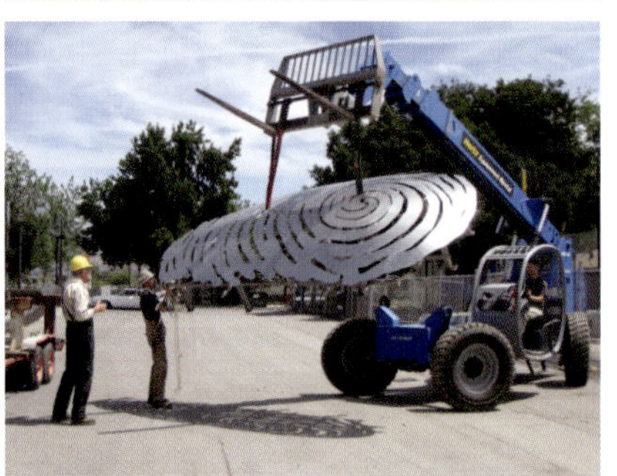
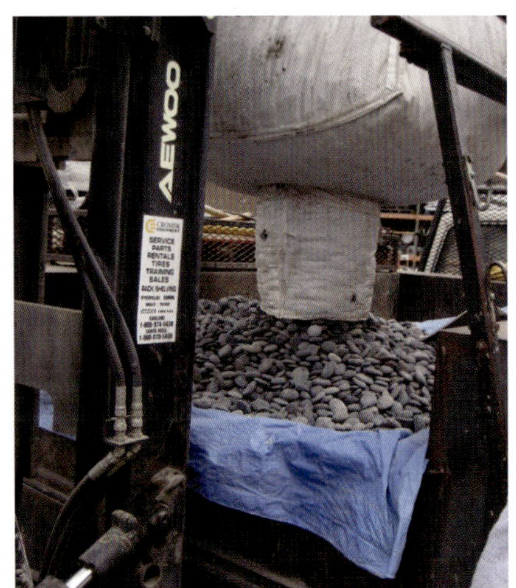
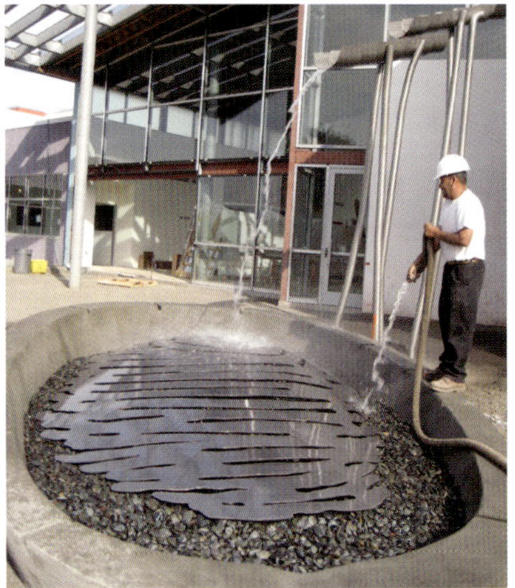
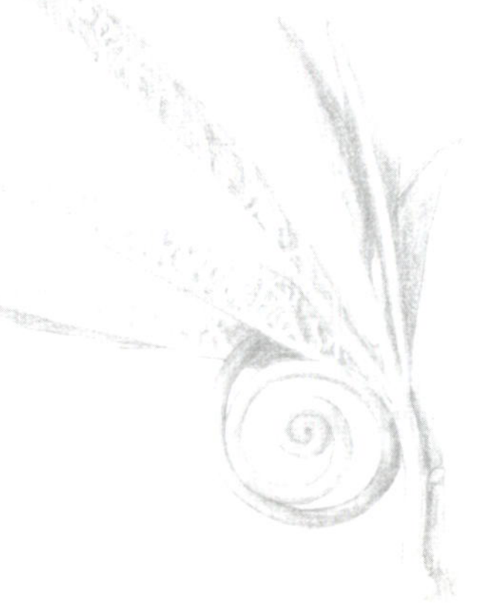

THUMBPRINT FILTER

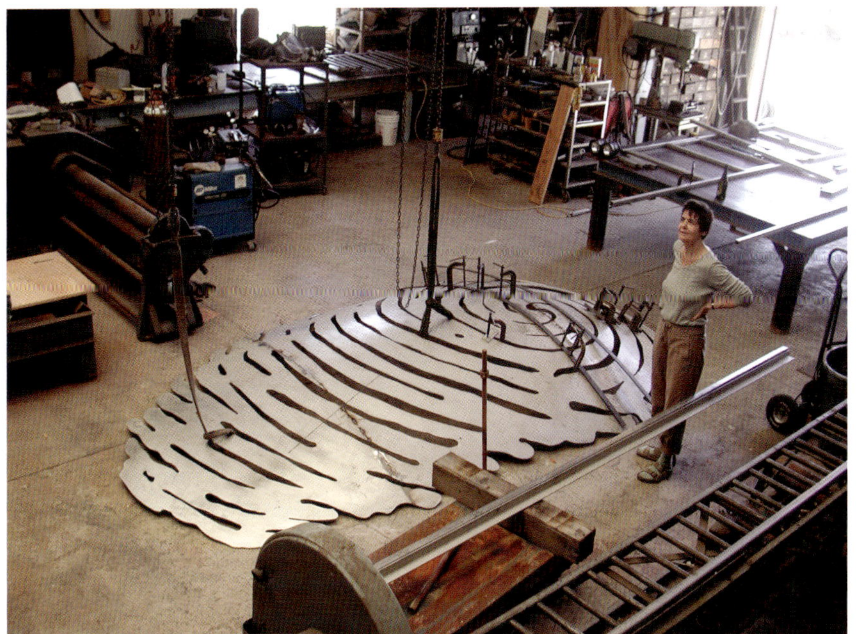

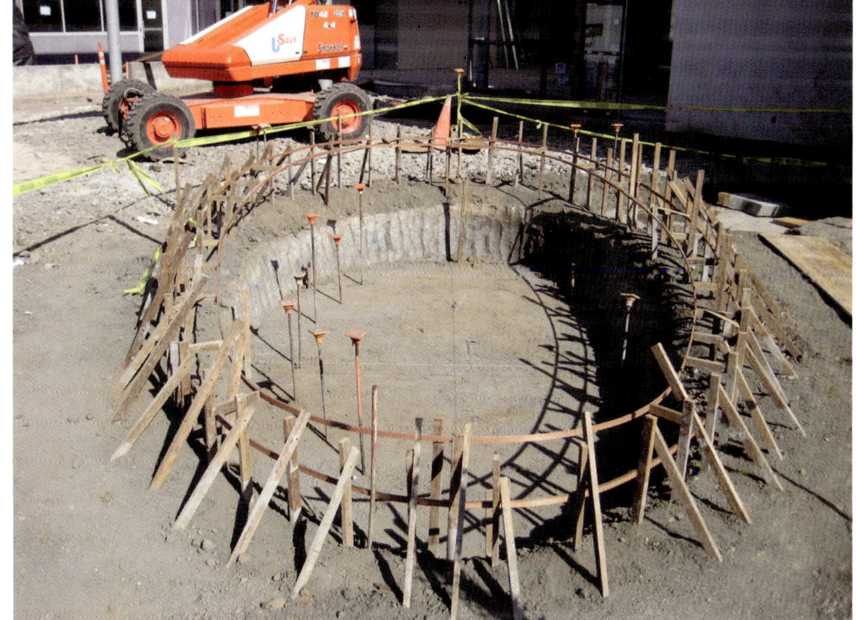

Left

Forming the concrete foundation began with roughly excavating the soil and forming the ellipse of the wall. Fabricating the thumbprint began with an 18" steel study. The stainless steel was rolled in several sections, which then required further shaping, cutting, and welding at Ellison Studio before being transported to the site.

Right

Jackie Brookner overseeing fabrication at Ellison Studio.

This preparatory work for supporting the concrete forms is as beautiful as it is meticulous.

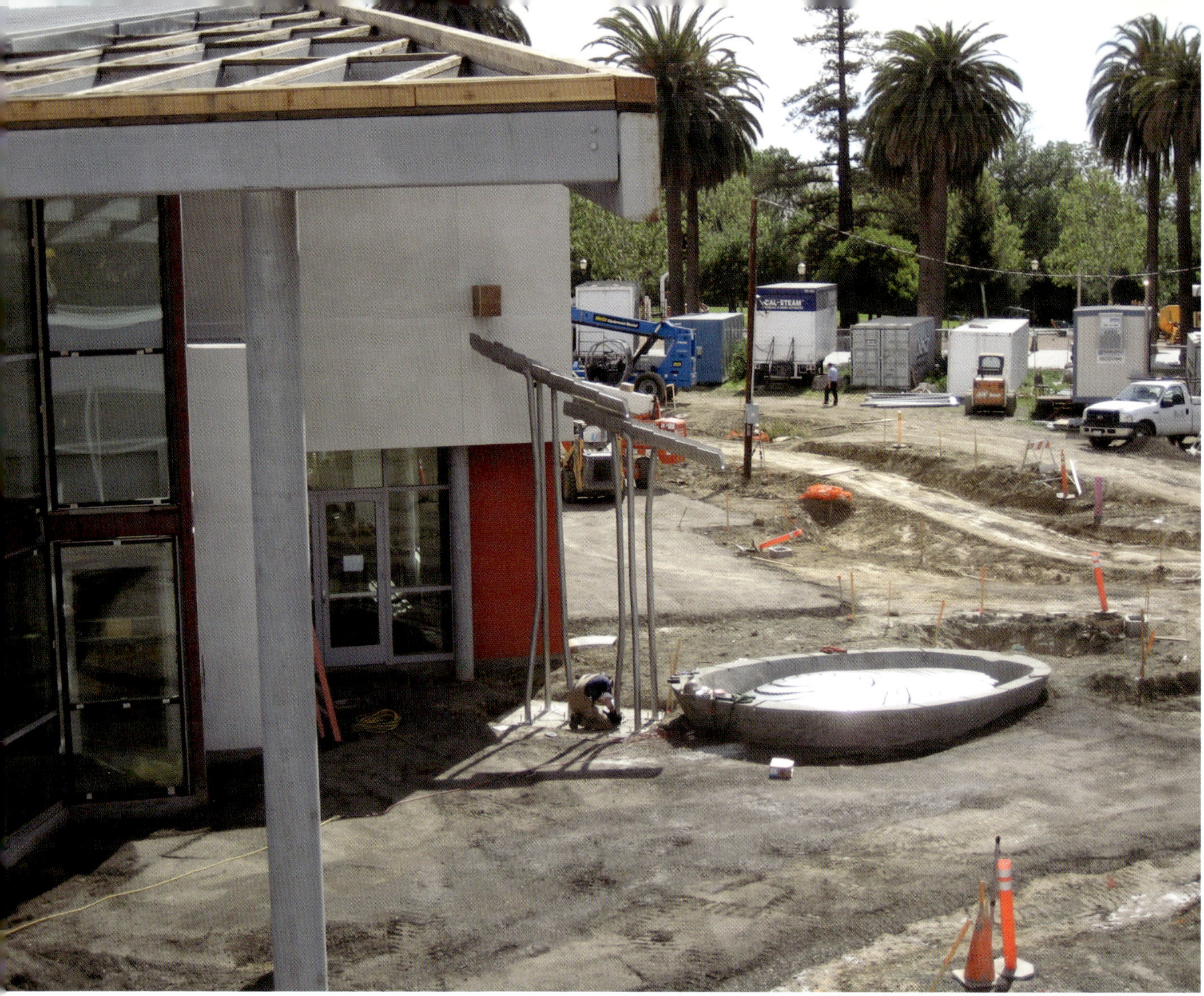

Anchoring the chutes and thumbprint to their foundations while the site was still under construction.

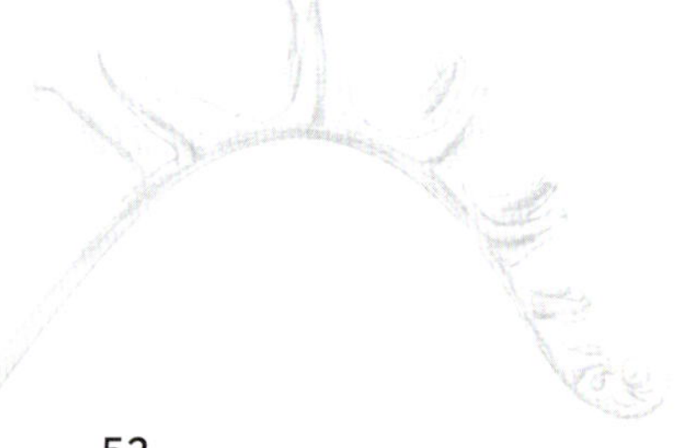

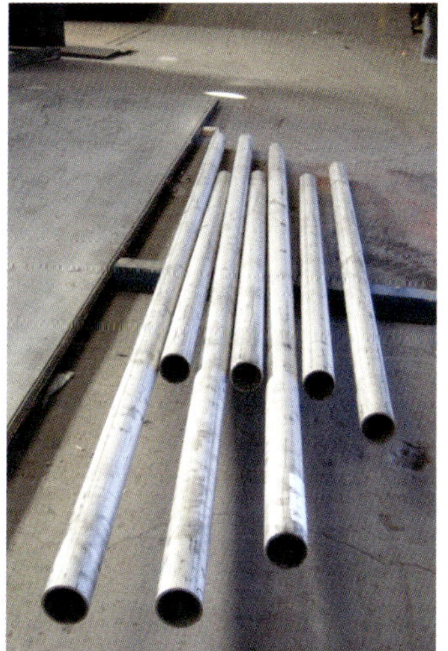
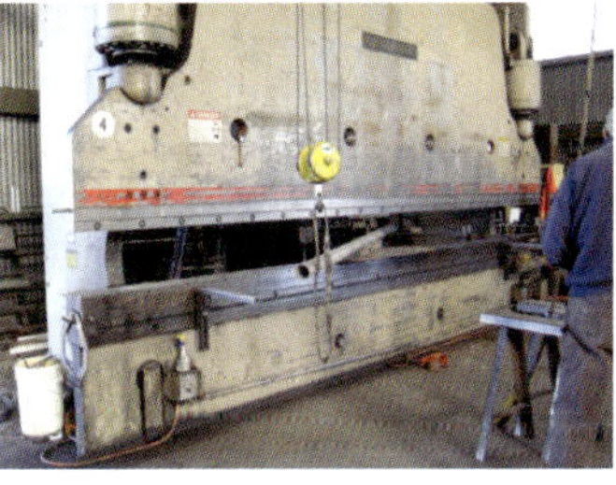
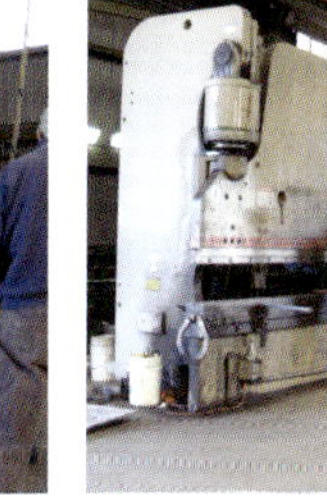
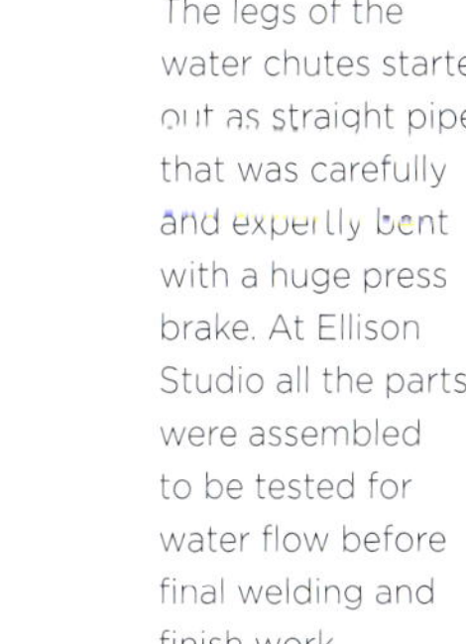

The legs of the water chutes started out as straight pipe that was carefully and expertly bent with a huge press brake. At Ellison Studio all the parts were assembled to be tested for water flow before final welding and finish work.

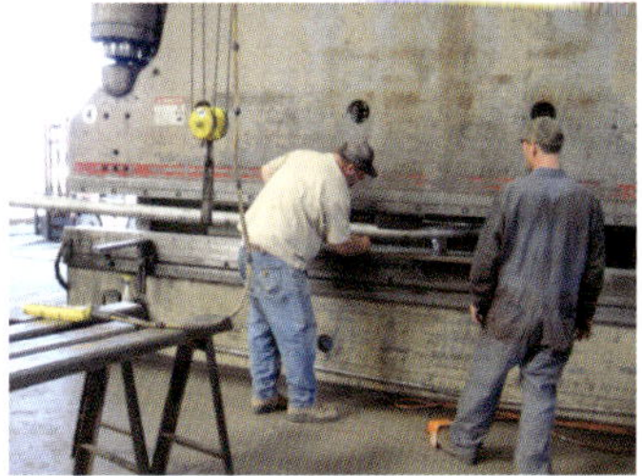
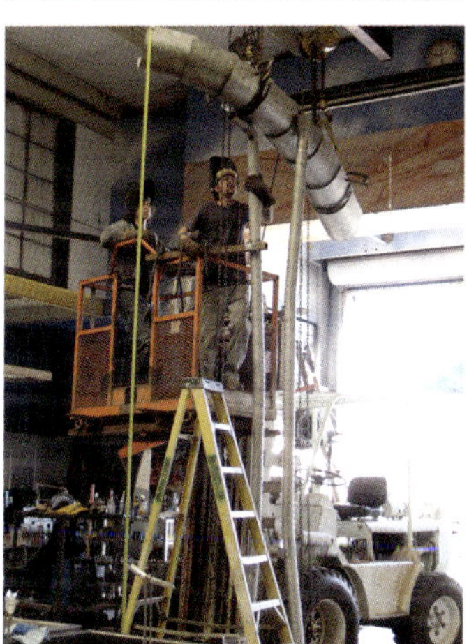
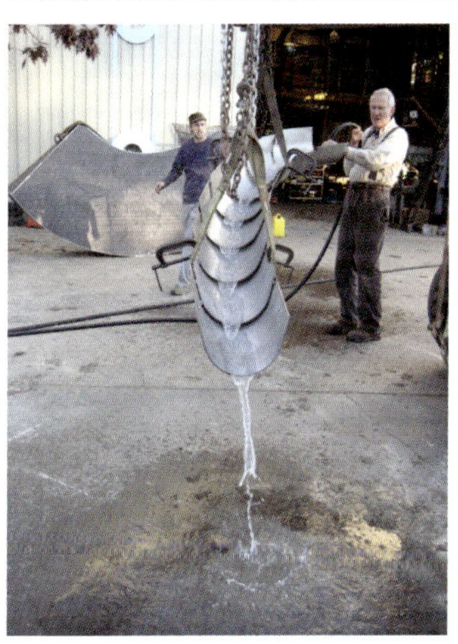
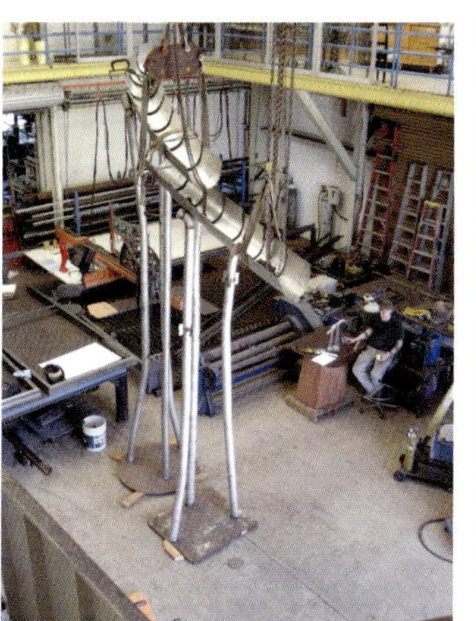
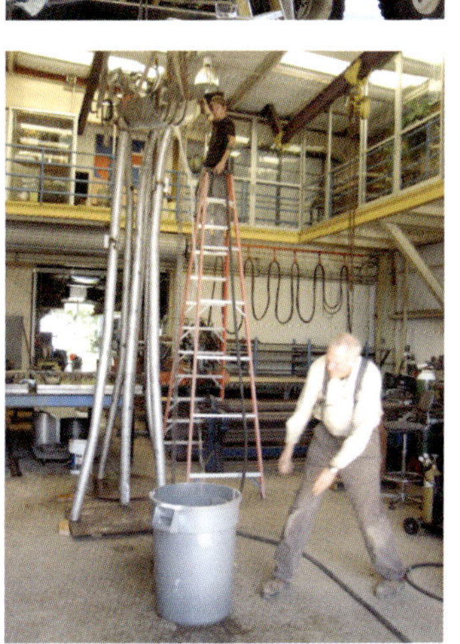
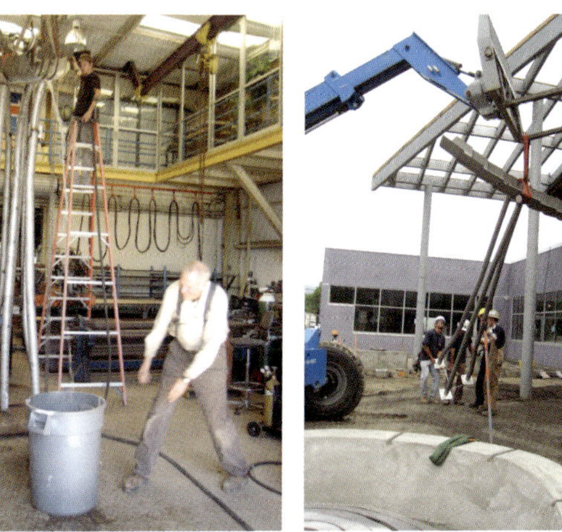
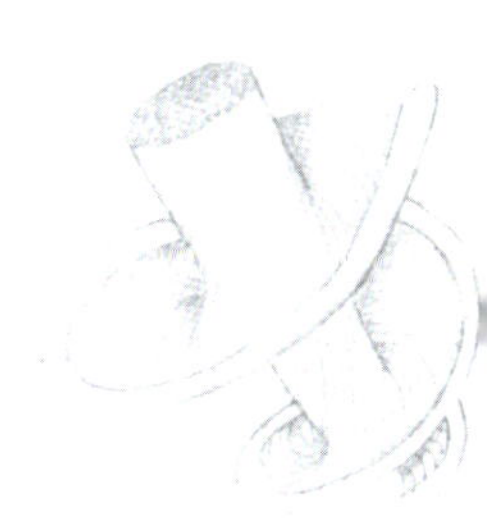

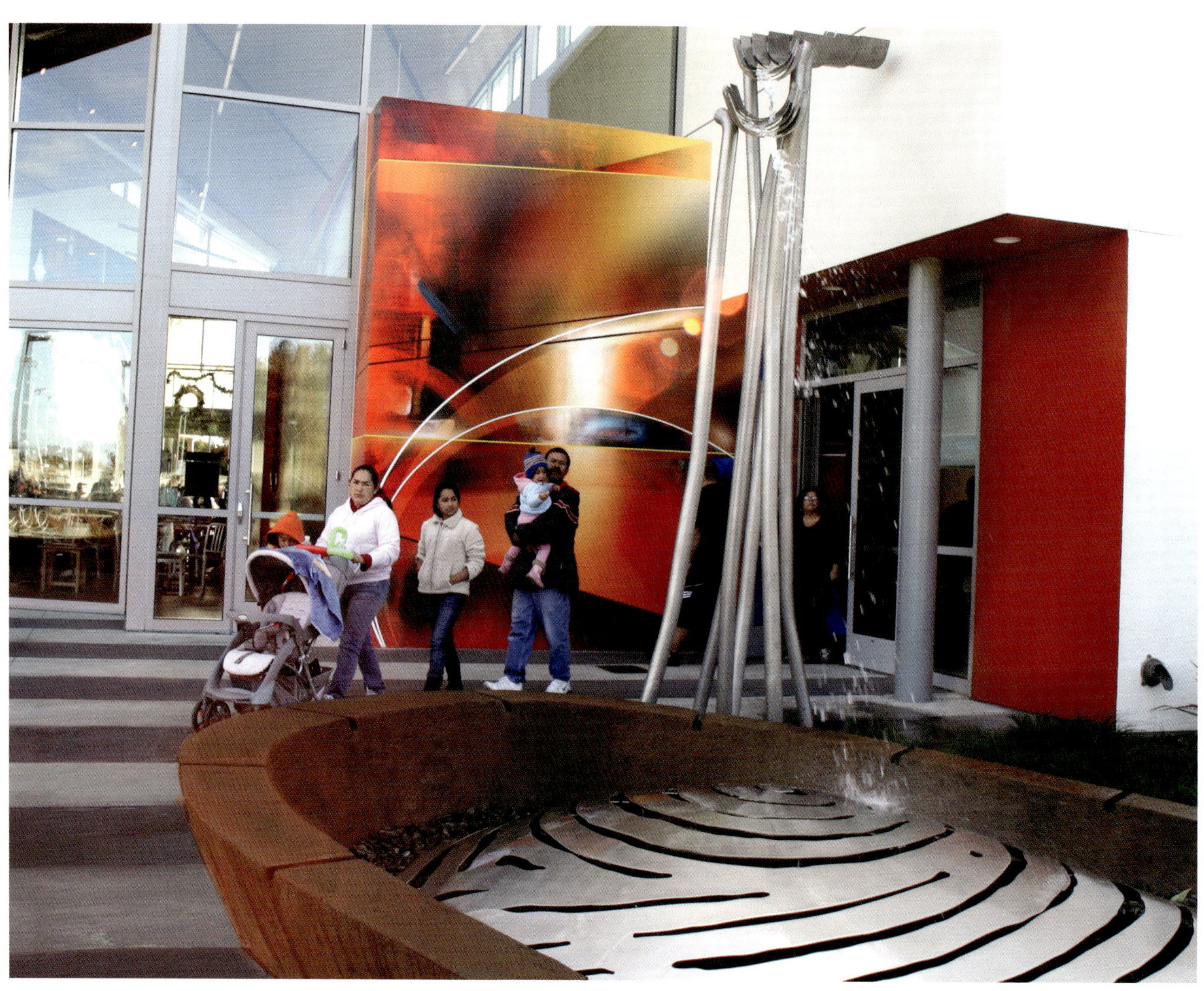

"There are hundreds of thousands of stems linking us to everything in the cosmos, and therefore we can be. Do you see the link between you and me? If you are not there, I am not here. That is certain. If you do not see it yet, look more deeply and I am sure you will see. As I said, this is not philosophy. You really have to see."

THICH NHAT HANH The Heart of Understanding

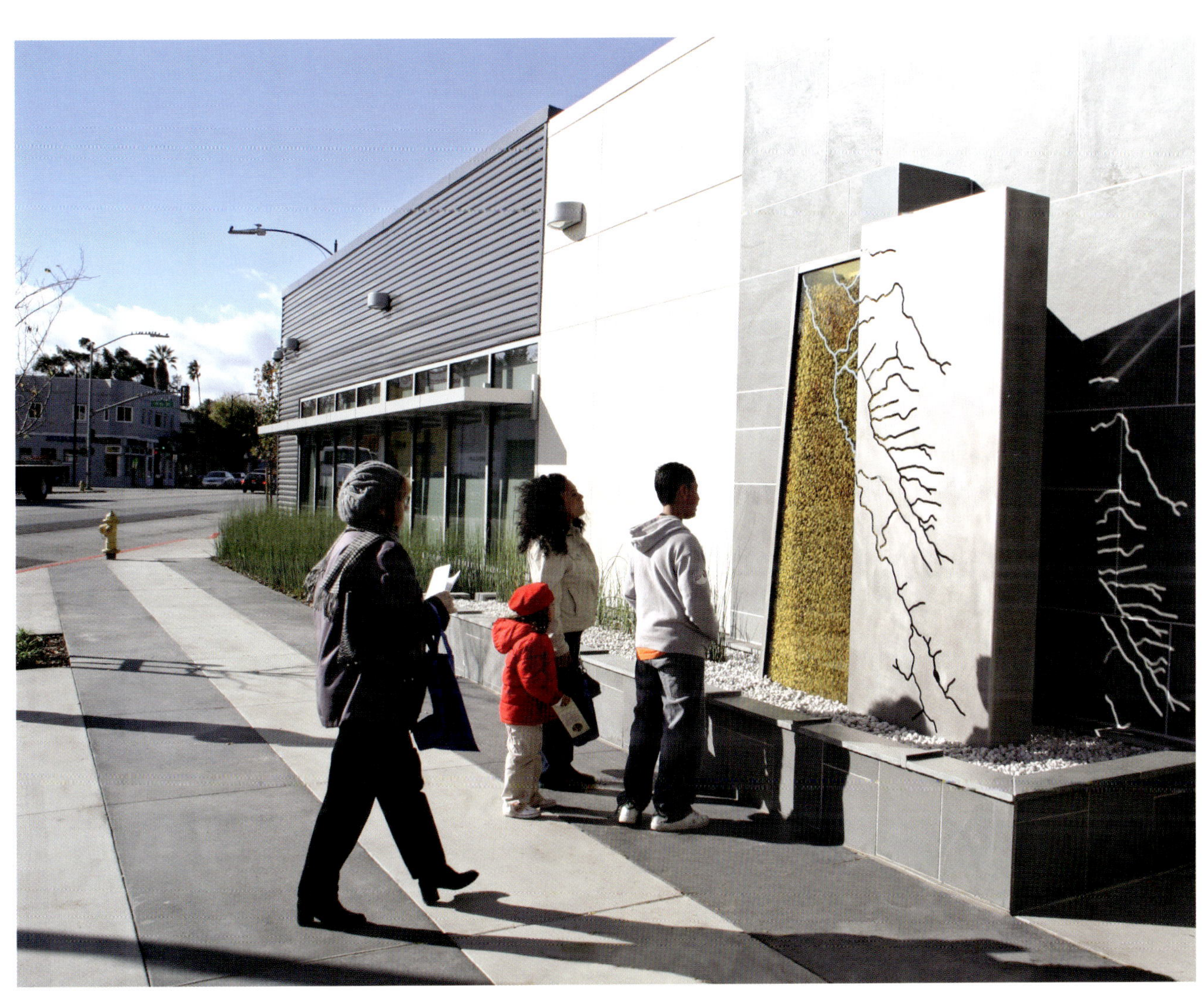

In resistance to environmental policies that claimed nature (e.g., wilderness) as a distinct and scientifically knowable subject apart from human relations, environmental justice politics have publicly produced nature as an open term around which to organize multiple and everyday claims to justice, freedom, and expression...This production of environmentalism leaves the subject of "the environment" open and legitimates the realm of appearance...

Ultimately, then, a green public culture is a realm in which the world can appear and be made meaningful in light of the opinions of multiple others thinking, reflecting, and imagining in each others' company. —Catriona Sandilands[1]

Fascinated and preoccupied by the visual character of the United States landscape and its relationship to emerging public values and conventions, the iconoclastic, peripatetic landscape observer, John Brinckerhoff (J. B.) Jackson spent most of his adult life looking, writing about what he saw, and inviting us to look and seek meaning in the amalgamation of settlements, spaces, structures, and natural systems in landscape. In spite of glaring historical and alarming contemporary examples of structural inequalities and social injustices, in his book *American Space: The Centennial Years* and many of his essays written as he crisscrossed the nation, Jackson examined concepts of equality and democracy represented in a grid system of land subdivision perhaps most optimistically and problematically represented by the Homestead Act of 1862 that divided the nation into a consistently applied patchwork of 160 acre plots. The generic, one-size-fits-all application of land use, now widely criticized for its complete disregard for topography, hydrology, and other environmental features and characteristics, was a graphic image of equality of opportunity—the relationship of citizenship and land ownership. But as Jackson indicates, as settlement and farming moved further west into the nation's Great Plains, the well-intended "assumption that all pieces of land of the same size had the same value, became totally unrealistic...The square of 160 acres, so reassuring in the more humid East, has no fixed value on the Plains; often it does not suffice to feed a half-dozen cows...So it was water in one

form or another that determined the size and location of a viable unit, whatever Washington supposed; it was topography that made land profitable or useless."[2]

More than 150 years later, our relationship to land, rain, and surface water, if more sophisticatedly managed or chronically ignored (as in the management of stormwater, for example) still raises questions and represents values and priorities regarding the use and availability of resources, our perception and understanding of natural systems and their relationship to public life and public good. While the United States government's 19th century Homestead Art promoted an expansion of the nation and individual equality based on land use and rugged individualism, a new environmental awareness of the intricate web of natural systems and human development has made issues of resource management matters of community concern. From municipal recycling programs, to the banning of pesticides by cities and communities, and the development of community-supported agricultural projects, an increasing attention to sustainable initiatives are more philosophically and instrumentally linked with public policies and individual choice.

For some contemporary environmentalists, J.B. Jackson was a scourge. As his collection of essays, *Landscape in Sight: Looking at America* confirms, his work was uncompromisingly about landscape—and looking at human initiatives through the land in an open-minded, often non-judgmental way.[3] He embraced Jeffersonian ideals of a democracy cultivated in an agrarian way of life that negotiated nature with the needs and aspirations of common people. In fact, Jackson criticized, if not condemned, Thoreau as a hopeless romantic who valued the virtues of wilderness and solitude over the facts of landscape and human intervention. Jackson squarely placed his view on the impact of the human presence in the world—on landscape. Seeing landscape as neither nature nor art (but, I suggest, perhaps with features of both) his writings analyzed the inscriptions on the landscape as signs of public values. His work, in particular his interest in the vitality of the vernacular, was independently philosophical and utterly pragmatic.

In their thoughtful, urgent introduction to the collection of essays in *Environmental Pragmatism*, editors Andrew Light and Eric Katz lament the precarious condition of the contemporary natural world and the chasm that exists between environmental philosophy and the actions and decisions of scientists, policy-makers, and (I would add) citizens. They speculate if ideas of application and agency embedded in American Pragmatism might generate a connective opportunity to galvanize philosophers and policy-makers in some of the most pressing environmental issues. Additionally, they ask more pointedly—and pragmatically—if philosophers (and I would add artists) can contribute to the intelligible presentation and resolution of environmental problems. "Do the traditions, history and skills of philosophical thought have any relevance to the development of environmental policy?"[4] Proposing that an idea of environmental pragmatism can meaningfully and instrumentally produce a fruitful dialectic of theory with practice and policy, they imagine an open-ended, open-minded, and ongoing environment of productive inquiry on sustainability, environmental problems—and solutions.

What partially separates us human architects from bees, however, is that we are now obliged (by our own achievements) to work out in the imagination as well as through discursive debates our individual and collective responsibilities not only to ourselves and each other but to all of those 'others' that comprise what we usually refer to as 'external' nature ('external', that is, to us)...We have long been powerful evolutionary agents through everything from plant and animal breeding, massive habitat modification, and rapid populations growth to the diffusion and mixing of species on a global scale...This in no way means that we are somehow 'outside of' metabolic or evolutionary constraints or invulnerable to natural forces. But we are in a position to consciously deploy the repertoire of evolved possibilities in radically different combinatorial ways." —David Harvey[5]

These ideas of land-use, biology, citizenship, equality, environmental ethics, and pragmatism are relevant, if not urgent, and provide an historical, intellectual, and aesthetic environment to consider the recent work of artist Jackie Brookner. Brookner has been deeply engaged in art concepts about environmental issues for more than fifteen years. With a particular interest in water remediation, Brookner has created a series of ecosystems that combine plants that cleanse and filter water with sculptural forms that frequently represent the human body—tongues, hands, and feet. These truncated parts of our anatomy, which we intimately understand as embodied experience, critically confront inoperable and unsustainable ways of envisioning ourselves and the world as discrete. In western culture, this model of discontinuity has served as a convenient, direct, if wildly inaccurate and unjustifiable representation of the alliance of human, non-human, and nature. Paradoxically, these disembodied parts serve as compelling, if not iconic, representations—points on another mental map with routes that connect human physiological intricacies with proliferating, intersecting, and interdependent processes of the natural world.

"Of Earth and Cotton" (1994-98) is a philosophical, poetic, and pragmatic project in Brookner's development as an artist. Traveling throughout the South, she met with women and men who farmed cotton in the 1930-40s. Without the aid of modern machinery, they were the workforce that picked cotton by hand, often in extreme conditions. She met these laborers and talked with them about their lives and labor. As they sat and talked, Brookner knelt before them and made life-sized, fully-formed portraits of their calloused, misshapen feet with the soil from fields in the area. The feet were sensitive representations of individuals and a disappearing way of life. But the feet, formed by work and age, also represented the conceptual joint where the verticality and movement of the human body met the horizontality and gravity of land and vast fields of cotton. The feet of these farmers are the functional intermediaries of agriculture and landscape—the confluence of natural phenomena and enterprising human intervention.

The new Roosevelt Community Center in San Jose, California is a facility sited in Roosevelt Park near the Coyote Creek. The creek is part of the vast watershed for the entire area, connecting all forms of underground hydrology and surface water that empty into San Francisco Bay. The community center serves as a space for many functions and activities for all ages. Its inclusive and open-ended program presents unusual challenges and opportunities for an artist working with the building and its site. There are many decisions for an artist; the work needs to communicate with a heterogeneous, constantly reconfigured group of occupants. The building, designed by Group 4 Architects, is seeking a LEED certification of gold. Issues of sustainability were embedded in the design process.

Brookner's project "Urban Rain" (2008) strikingly connects the new building to its immediate site, as well as a largely invisible watershed. The artist uses stormwater as both a raw material to exploit and the problem to solve producing a fascinating feedback loop of aesthetic decisions and ecological imperatives. At the north and south entries to the community center, she has installed two inter-related works that do, in fact, "work". Adjacent to the south entry, "The Coyote Creek Filter" directs rainwater from the building's roof through a scupper box positioned above a glass filter. In the filter, rocks slow and delay the movement of the water. As water passes between the rocks, it is filtered by micro-organisms on the surface of the rocks. Generally, this natural process of filtration occurs underground and out of sight, but Brookner deliberately "presents" this simple, cleansing process to the buildings' users. She reveals or "shows" people something that is commonplace in the natural world, yet generally hidden or unobserved.

Paradoxically, when artists seek to reproduce or re-enact natural processes a high level of conspicuous artifice is inevitable. On the surfaces of the glass and stainless steel surfaces of the filtrations system, Brookner has inscribed the rhizomatic system of the Coyote Creek and tributaries that constitute the area's watershed and connect to the San Francisco Bay. The process of filtration at the building's entry is expansively contextualized within an intricately-connected ecological system. On the other side of the building, "The Chutes and Thumbprint Filter" presents another path of water filtration. Here, rainwater from the roof passes through a scupper box, travels through chutes, and drains into a shallow horizontal pool where it is slowly filtered, again by micro-organisms on rocks, before it is released into the ground. In addition to the contrasting configuration of the filtration apparatus, Brookner presents an alternative iconography. The pattern of the stainless steel pool is based on a human thumbprint whose radiating lines of sensation and personal identification connect with the spiral movement of water, winds, and other natural currents and movement. While at the south entry viewers apprehend a panoramic inscription of the tributaries and topography of the Coyote Creek regional watershed, the image of the filtration system on the north side of the building connects the intimate scale of our own anatomy to the structure of the hydrological cycle in the natural world. In tandem, both filtration elements of "Urban Rain" alternately contract and dilate, offering opportunities for concentrated focus with a more expansive representation of our relational complicity with the natural world.

> *Relations between scales must be understood because our responsibilities to nature and to our own species being comprise actions that vary from the micro preservation of habitat diversities in hedgerows and in nooks and crannies of gardens through regional issues like deteriorating water resources and tropospheric ozone concentrations to the hugely complicated global issues of stratospheric ozone depletion, resource degradation, maintenance of biodiversity, and global warming. Dialectical utopianism has to incorporate such issues within its compass, for this is the ecological world we have to change as we seek to change ourselves. —David Harvey[6]*

How are things revealed to us? And how does the process of observation make the world more intelligible to us? In these questions, we identify or describe the significant, if not fundamental, role of the artist. Artists often take what is invisible, indiscernible, or overlooked and make it accessible and perceptible, if only transitionally and sometimes tenuously. Admittedly, it is difficult to "see"—to witness—the actual process of filtration and the purifying activities of micro-organisms, but viewers are presented an opportunity to encounter conceptually—and procedurally—how something as obvious as water captured from a roof, rather than as random runoff that collects pollutants from parking lots and other paved surfaces before it enters the watershed, can be mediated and manipulated to enter a hydrological system in a less compromised, more "natural" condition.

My central argument has been that the composite image— variously instantiated as a visual formula, emblem, symbol, and correlational montage ... is the prototype for how we integrate sensation and concept...Openwork, mesh, lattice, grid as well as opaque connecting patterns, specifically, create an interface where the prismatic facets of the environment get visibly superimposed or set down side by side our qualitative sensations. This dovetailing makes us not only conscious of ourselves as subject but as an object... Self-consciousness and context-consciousness are shown to be inextricable. —Barbara Maria Stafford[7]

Brookner is involved in a revelatory practice that seeks to disclose and show biological processes without simplifying or demystifying their complexity. She works through an art of extraction, presenting selected parts or elements—a small channel of water, a biological feature, a part of the human body—that represent open-ended complexity and inter-connectivity. While she, of necessity, extracts, she never isolates. As Stafford suggests about the endless potential of images, Brookner's work expounds an expansive register that spans the dynamics of subjectivity to the incalculable dimensions of context.

If J. B. Jackson was interested in the images of (human) work in the landscape, Stafford, from her perspective of art and neuroscience, examines the work of images. "The cognitive work of images does not just make our complex environment simpler to digest. It makes aspects of the world perceptually salient and cognitively distinctive for us."[8] In contrasting ways, these independent, interdisciplinary intellectuals examine and expose the meaning and consequence of observation—how intelligibility emanates in the world and through the mind and body. As an artist, Brookner makes things and images in and on environments that, with a poetic, self-contained pragmatism, reveal small, salient slices of the workings of the world. If "seeing is believing" is no longer an inevitable equation in a highly mediated culture, Brookner enacts a dialectic of seeing and attentiveness. If the parts, fragments, and iconography do not create a whole, they activate contemplation that seeks connection. Through Brookner's work we are asked to consider how the world which we share is represented. Art is never an end in itself; its appearance is always (and all ways) a means of inquiry with imagination.

Reality is different from, and more than, the totality of facts and events, which, anyhow, is unascertainable. Who says what is ...always tells a story, and in this story the particular facts lose their contingency and acquire some humanly comprehensible meaning. — Hannah Arendt[9]

Patricia C. Phillips

January 2009

Patricia Phillips is an independent writer on art, public art, and how contemporary art practices intersect with other fields. She is professor and chair of the Department of Art at Cornell University.

Notes

1. Catriona Sandilands, "Opinionated Natures: Towards a Green Civic Culture," in Ben A. Minteer and Bob Pepperman Taylor (ed.). *Democracy and the Claims of Nature: Critical Perspectives for a New Century* (New York: Rowan & Littlefield Publishers, Inc., 2002) 128-29.
2. John Brinckerhoff Jackson, "Excerpt from American Space: The Centennial Years", *Landscape in Sight: Looking at America* (New Haven: Yale University Press, 1997), 155
3. Ibid.
4. Andrew Light and Eric Katz (ed.) Environmental Pragmatism (New York: Routledge, 1996) 1
5. David Harvey. *Spaces of Hope* (Berkeley: University of California Press, 2000) 213-14
6. Harvey, 220
7. Barbara Maria Stafford. *Echo Objects: The Cognitive Work of Images* (Chicago: University of Chicago Press, 2007) 206
8. Stafford, 207
9. Hannah Arendt. *Between Past and Future* (Hammondsworth, Middlesex: Penguin, 1963) 261-62

Beyond its aesthetic qualities, and its elegant functionality, the most important characteristic of Jackie Brookner's latest work is its symbolic optimism to infrastructure planners in a world of burgeoning populations, growing resource scarcity, and unstable economic conditions. These professionals are responsible for finding cost effective ways to meet the water, energy, waste disposal, transportation and other urgent needs of a growing and urbanizing world under increasingly stringent environmental and social constraints. The pressure is especially intense for the planners of water infrastructure, whose designs intimately link the engineered, natural, and social dimensions of our world.

Previous eras of urbanization also created great water infrastructure needs. During the 19th and early 20th centuries, for example, increased population density led to contamination of local water sources, and the need to appropriate increasingly distant tracts of originally rural land for municipal supplies. Complex networks of tunnels, aqueducts, and channels were designed to convey this water to thirsty population centers. Improved accessibility increased consumption- and the amount of water that was wasted. Rooftops, roadways, and other impervious surfaces disconnected aquifers from the atmosphere, converting incident precipitation immediately into runoff. Downstream from the city, storm drains, ditches, canals, and sewer lines were designed to efficiently collect, convey, and dispose of "waste" waters (runoff and domestic sewage), an engineering gesture not unlike the one that ultimately also determined the fate of our solid waste. Conflict emerged at multiple scales, as various stakeholders laid claims to this precious resource, almost always at the expense of natural systems.

While fundamental to the development of what we today consider functional cities, this kind of water infrastructure also significantly reduced the ability of ecosystems to provide essential goods and services. Unsustainable rates of extraction, for example, permanently reduced natural stocks in lakes and underground aquifers that had taken millennia to accumulate. Without the transpiration of plants, paved surfaces increased air temperatures, while also inhibiting the ability of those same landscapes to absorb rainfall and

prevent floods, and pollution significantly reduced the vitality of valuable fisheries.

Although these impacts have been well documented, the design philosophy responsible for them persists. In part this is because the ongoing vitality of many cities is only possible through a continuation of the unsustainable water management practices that made them possible in the first place. The haste with which urgent new water infrastructure projects are planned and undertaken is also a factor, as it often leaves designers with very little time to devise and test alternative approaches.

The good news is that more sustainable management approaches are, nonetheless, gaining in popularity. Known as green infrastructure, low impact development, or a range of other terms, these old and new technologies seek to integrate development into the local hydrologic cycle, with multiple and far-reaching benefits. Where appropriate and feasible, the harvesting and capture of precipitation, for example, can eliminate the need for expensive drainage infrastructure, while at the same time also minimize the likelihood of downstream flooding. A reduction in the fraction of precipitation that becomes runoff also reduces the occurrences of soil erosion and nonpoint source pollution. The design of special areas that promote infiltration can help to recharge the aquifer and raise the local water table; and a higher water table, in turn, is more accessible to plants, easier to access with wells, and contributes to higher base flows in local streams and rivers during dry weather. If harvested rainwater

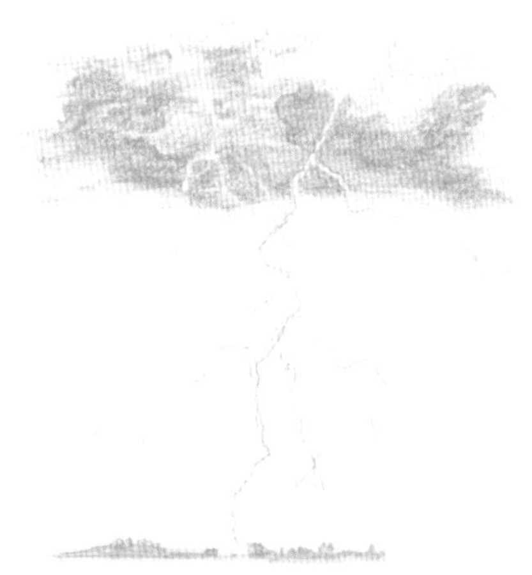

is used in lieu of piped drinking water for non-potable uses, the same practice will also reduce water infrastructure needs upstream of the development. When less water is piped out of a basin, more water is available to sustain critical environmental flows or to irrigate agricultural lands within it. These resources can also become the domestic supply for yet unserved communities, and our world still has plenty of them.

The elegance and ease with which Jackie Brookner demonstrates this new elevated purpose of water infrastructure at the Roosevelt Community Center is what makes the work so significant and inspiring. In a beautiful marriage of form and function, water harvested from the roof of the building is very deliberately directed into intricately designed glass and rock filters, before it is almost magically infiltrated into the ground. The rock filter, elevated above the ground surface, makes visible natural processes that although usually unseen, will always shape our environment. The meandering etching in the filter's glass wall is symbolic of the real-world, non-linear complexity of these processes, and yet also testament to their abstract beauty. On the other side of the building, a series of chutes purposefully discharge roof runoff, a product of this and many other developments, into a thumbprint shaped infiltration zone. In this case the discharge is benign, but the thumbprint is a reminder that all of our actions ultimately have an impact. Together, these gestures demonstrate that with a few subtle changes in design thinking, the relationship between the built and natural environment can be entirely transformed.

In his book, *The End of Nature*, Bill McKibben differentiates today's environmental crises from all previous ones by its global pervasiveness. In the 19th century, most migrating birds still paused for food in the same network of wetlands and estuaries frequented by the previous thousand generations. In the 1920's, an urban family could still travel a few hours by wagon to escape the disease and noise of the city. In the 1960's, an adventurer could still surround himself in mind-boggling biodiversity by simply traveling to some of the more remote corners of any continent. But today, not a square meter plot remains where the effects of human activity, in the form of climate change, cannot be detected.

The debilitating impact that this sobering reality can have on a humble and well intentioned designer is formidable. But just as the end of life for the caterpillar is the beginning of life for the butterfly, a modification of our purpose as designers can transform this sense of doom into one of hope. My intention here is not to trivialize the effects of human induced climate change, but rather to remind the reader of the power of transformative thinking—the kind that Brookner's work exemplifies and evokes. Her work challenges us to think about what we value and why, and encourages us to articulate these values in our actions and in what we make. If virgin resources are becoming scarce, then it is "wasted" resources that we must learn how to recycle. If natural watersheds have become urban watersheds, then it is urban watersheds that merit our attention. Without an adjustment of the rudder, the honest designers among us can easily lose the motivation to keep rowing. But by adjusting the goals of our designs as Brookner has, we can with clear conscious continue to contribute to human development.

The integration of systems like those built into many of Brookner's projects—systems that capture, treat, and productively utilize water sources conventionally labeled as "waste" is symbolic of the more sustainable development trajectories that are very much within reach. To be sure, this transformation of how we design community will not be simple. Many practical, political, and philosophical problems need still to be addressed. Despite these challenges, "Urban Rain" encourages us to address the significant problems of our generation with a shifted perspective. Through careful design, many problems can be converted into solutions, buildings can be integrated into landscapes, and humans can rejoin nature.

Franco Montalto

Dr. Montalto is the "Sustainable Engineering" professor in the Department of Civil, Architectural, and Environmental Engineering of Drexel University in Philadelphia. He is also the President and Founder of eDesign Dynamics, LLC a New York City based environmental engineering firm specializing in green infrastructure, and in the restoration and design of natural systems for habitat, treatment, and other benefits.

ACKNOWLEDGMENTS

I am grateful to so many people whose expertise and assistance has been essential to the success of this project. I thank the Environmental Services Department for their help and enthusiasm throughout. This book and the project as it is would not exist without the support of ESD's Melody Tovar and Anastazia Aziz. Equally fundamental has been guidance from the San Jose Public Art Program staff. My gratitude to Barbara Goldstein for her oversight and thoughtful vision of the potentials of Public Art, to Joe Saxe for his caring and effective project management, and to JenJoy Roybal for her work in the early stages. Group 4 Architects helped figure out our areas of mutual interest, and Jonathan Hartman graciously addressed my endless questions and concerns. Benjamin Gonzales from the Department of Public Works is the liaison extraordinaire, an invaluable help at smoothing out the bumps and ensuring the best outcomes for all,. I also thank Kimmy Chen of David Gates Landscape Architects and John Urdahl of David Smith Electric.

It has been a true gift to work with such talented and patient fabricators, artists and contractors as Robert Ellison and Josh Spaulding of Robert Ellison Studio, Mark McAndrews of MPM Concrete, Dorothy Lenahan of Lenahan Glass, Barbara Derix and Jocelyn Shoup of Derix Glass, Van Bebber Steel and Craig Charbonneau. Under their work lay the drawings of Steve Petrushka and engineering of Tim Hyde. It has been a pleasure to work on the design of this book with Birgit Wick who somehow found order in my piles of documentation, and with photographer Cesar Rubio.

I am deeply grateful to Patricia Phillips and Franco Montalto. The depth and thoughtfulness of their writing have opened up new layers of meaning for me, and I hope for others. And to my dear (no longer new) friends, Kathie Zaretsky, Jonathan Karpf, and Diana Pompelly Bates, who welcomed me so generously into their homes and lives in San Jose. Finally I thank my parents, Sidney and Isabelle Weinstein, for their love and support, and for the gift of life.

—Jackie Brookner

City of San Jose

Mayor
Chuck Reed

City Council
Pete Constant, District 1
Ash Kalra, District 2
Sam Liccardo, District 3
Kansen Chu, District 4
Nora Campos, District 5
Pierluigi Oliverio District 6
Madison Nguyen, District 7
Rose Herrera, District 8
Vice Mayor Judy Chirco, District 9
Nancy Pyle, District 10

Arts Commission
Michael Martin, Chair
Chris Esparza, Chair, Ad Hoc Outreach Committee
Lisa Gonzales, EdD
Rick Holden
Charles Lauer
Dennis Martin
Patricia Borba McDonald, Chair, Public Art Committee
Nathan Montgomery
Timothy Shannon
Walter Soellner
Ruth Tunstall-Grant
Bobby Yount, Chair, Program Committee

With Thanks To:

City Manager
Anastazia Aziz
Ashwini Kantak

Environmental Services
James Downing
Mary Morse
Melody Tovar

Group 4 Architects
Jonathan Hartman

Parks Recreation and Neighborhood Services Department
Marie Alberry–Hawkins

Department of Public Works
Benjamin Gonzales

West Coast Contractors
Diego Rocamora
Pete Stringer

Office of Cultural Affairs
Barbara Goldstein
Joe Saxe

CREDITS

ORO editions
Publishers of Architecture, Art, and Design
Gordon Goff – Publisher
USA: PO Box 998, Pt Reyes Station, CA 94056
Asia: Block 8, Lorong Bakar Batu #02-04, Singapore 348743
www.oroeditions.com
info@oroeditions.com

Project Coordination: Joanne Tan and Davina Tjandra
Production: Gordon Goff and Joanne Tan
Color Separation & Printing: ORO editions Pte Ltd
Covers: 360 gsm artcard with matt lamination
Text Paper: 157 gsm premium matt artpaper printed 4c using soy inks with
an off-line water based gloss spot varnish applied to all photographs

Printed in Singapore by ORO *group ltd*.

Design: Birgit Wick, wickdesignstudio.com
Typeface: Gotham
Drawings © 2009 by Jackie Brookner
All photos by Jackie Brookner except for the following:
Cover, page 2, 4, 12, 13, 15, 17, 18, 19, 20, 21 © 2009 by Cesar Rubio
Page 43 © 2009 by Terry Iacuzzo
Photo page 63 © 2009 by Marjorie Vecchio
Essay pages 10-55 © 2009 Jackie Brookner
Essay pages 56-59 © 2009 Patricia C. Phillips
Essay pages 60-61 © 2009 Franco Montalto

The public art project and the printing was funded by the City of San Jose
Office of Cultural Affairs and Environmental Services Department
365 South Market Street, San Jose, CA 95113, (408) 277-5144
http://www.sanjoseculture.org/?pid=4100

ORO *editions* has made every effort to minimize the overall carbon
footprint of this project. As part of this goal ORO *editions* and its clients,
in association with Global ReLeaf and American Forestry, have made an
ongoing arrangement to plant two trees for each and every tree used in
the manufacturing of the paper for this book.

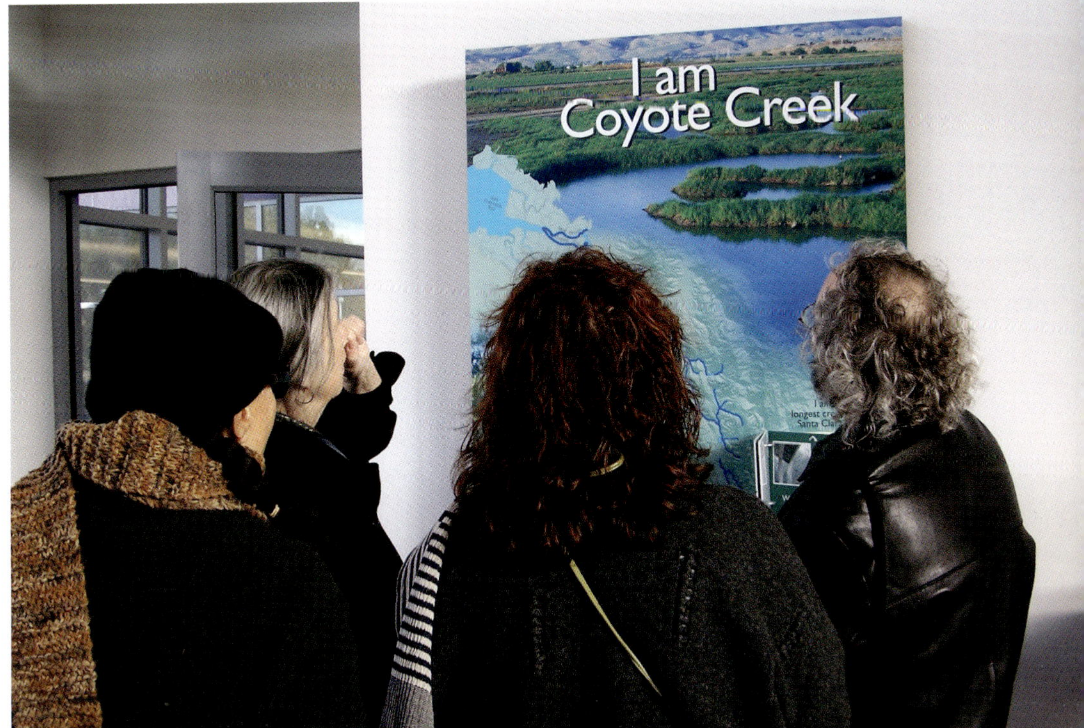

Visitors at
opening day,
December 13